Classic Restaurants
OF
WICHITA

DENISE NEIL

AMERICAN PALATE

Published by American Palate
A Division of The History Press
Charleston, SC
www.historypress.com

Copyright © 2021 by Denise Neil
All rights reserved

First published 2021

Manufactured in the United States

ISBN 9781467146975

Library of Congress Control Number: 2021938392

Notice: The information in this book is true and complete to the best of our knowledge. It is offered without guarantee on the part of the author or The History Press. The author and The History Press disclaim all liability in connection with the use of this book.

This book is dedicated to Mary Anne and Dennis Neil, who chose me, encouraged me and supported me through my journalism studies and beyond. I'm lucky to be your daughter.

Also to Hal Lister, who I never met but who gave me the journalism gene.

Contents

Acknowledgements   7
Introduction   9

PART I. WICHITA'S FIRST RESTAURANTS
1870–1915: Saloons, Chili Parlors and a
     Fred Harvey House   15
1916–1929: Tearooms, Cafeterias and the Rise
     of the Chop Suey Palace   21
1930–1939: Home-Style Cooking, Diners and
     White Castle's Departure   37
1940–1949: North Broadway Nightclubs and
     Barbecue to Go   53
1950–1959: Drive-Ins, Sit-Ins and the Start of Pizza Hut   69

PART II. THE MODERN DINING SCENE EMERGES
1960–1969: Steaks, Fondue and Beef on Buns   89
1970–1979: Fern Bars, Supper Clubs and That
     Old English Flair   101
1980–1989: Fine Dining, Fun Dining and the
     Early Days of Old Town   129
Still Serving after All These Years   144

Sources   153
Index   155
About the Author   159

Acknowledgements

When I first told *Wichita Eagle* editor Michael Roehrman that I'd been asked to write a book about iconic Wichita restaurants, I presented it as no big deal—something I would toss together during my free time after work. He laughed and asked me, "Have you ever written a book before?"

Now I have, and of course, Michael was correct that it would, in fact, be a big deal. I'd like to thank him for granting me permission to take this project on and for always being supportive of my restaurant reporting at the *Wichita Eagle*. The same goes for my direct editor while I was writing this, Jean Hays, who always gave me the freedom to follow my reporting instincts.

I'm most grateful to the many descendants of Wichita restaurant pioneers who agreed to meet with me or take my calls and who then dug through their family photo albums and scrapbooks to find many of the photos and mementos included in these pages. I'm so thankful that they trusted me to remove these valuable relics from their homes with just a verbal promise that I'd take good care of them and return them soon. (I did.)

My access to the *Wichita Eagle*'s and *Wichita Beacon*'s paper and digital archives during this project was invaluable, and although they're gone, I feel even more thankful now than I ever have for the talents of my newspaper predecessors Kathleen Kelly, Diane Lewis and Fran Kentling. These amazing women wrote hundreds of stories about Wichita restaurants during the '60s, '70s, '80s and '90s and did a perfect job of capturing what made those places so special. I hope that decades from now, some other journalist finds my restaurant writing as valuable. Diane and Fran, I will miss you always.

I also must mention Wichita historian Beccy Tanner, whose articles I referenced frequently throughout this project. I've only recently begun to fully appreciate and share her passion for Wichita's past.

The Wichita–Sedgwick County Historical Museum generously agreed to share several photos from its collection, which I think makes this book an even more complete document. I've always appreciated and admired the museum's executive director, Eric Cale, and its curator of collections, Jami Frazier Tracy. The *Wichita Eagle* also allowed me to dig deep in the archives and use photos of old Wichita restaurants that haven't been seen in years.

Joe Stumpe gave me invaluable tips for navigating this process, which he has already survived once with his excellent book *Wicked Wichita*. And Robin Macy gave me a huge gift when she offered me an extended stay at her gorgeous Bartlett Arboretum in Belle Plaine, Kansas, so I could push through the final pages of this project.

I have to mention the amazing Facebook group "If you grew up in wichita, ks, then you remember," which has nearly forty-five thousand members, many of whom are just as enthusiastic about Wichita history, and Wichita restaurant history in particular, as I am. If ever I needed to fill in some blanks about a restaurant from the past, I could always find ample descriptions and musings on that page.

Thank you to Suzanne Perez and Carrie Rengers for their proofreading prowess, as well as for their friendship and humor, and to my BFF and photo friend Jaime Green, who not only proofread pages but also helped gain permission for me to use historic *Wichita Eagle* photos.

Finally, a million thank-yous to my daughter, Alexis, and stepdaughter, Helen, for being patient during the months I was somewhat absent from your lives while I worked on this. And an extra special thank-you to my husband, photojournalist extraordinaire Travis Heying, who scanned numerous photos and menus for me, color corrected and resized all my images and provided technical and moral support as I hunched behind my monitor for months. I love you guys. Now it's time to catch up on our shows! (And our cleaning.)

Introduction

I started writing about restaurants for the *Wichita Eagle* as a twenty-seven-year-old reporter who loved to eat out and who was becoming a pretty competent home cook, inspired by my co-workers Diane Lewis and Fran Kentling, who'd been high-profile Wichita foodies for decades.

My first restaurant review was published in the paper in October 2000. I gave C. Bass, a seafood restaurant by future Freddy's Frozen Custard & Steakburgers co-founder Scott Redler, a positive write-up, and I praised its "perfectly fried crab cakes"; "rich, thick and flavorful" cioppino; and "beautifully presented daily fish specials." That restaurant lasted only six months before Redler changed the concept. But considering where Redler is today—helping oversee from his Wichita office a booming four-hundred-plus restaurant chain that he and his co-founder recently sold in what one must assume was a multimillion-dollar deal—I think things turned out okay for him.

When it disappeared, C. Bass joined a long, long list of Wichita restaurants that existed for a time, earned fans, fed locals—gave them a place to celebrate anniversaries, birthdays, engagements, Friday nights—and then closed and faded into memories.

But if there's one thing I've learned over my two decades of writing about restaurants in this city, it's that restaurants never really disappear. They live on in the hearts of people who loved them, and the best ones inspire nostalgia that endures for decades.

Wichitans have always loved to eat out, from the early days when the restaurant scene was a collection of saloons and lunch counters, to the burger stands of the '50s, through the swank private supper clubs of the '70s and the Lebanese restaurant explosion of the 1980s and 1990s. Behind the scenes, there have always been hardworking folks who wanted to feed people, and some have done it extremely well.

I learned early on as a restaurant reporter which historic restaurants Wichitans held in the highest regard. If I ever polled readers about the restaurants they remembered, the same names were repeated over and over: Innes Tea Room. Fife and Drum. Fairland Cafe. Abe's. Doc's. The Looking Glass. Portobello Road. Cafe Chantilly. Albert's. Even decades later, people could recall in detail specific dishes they loved, specific occasions they celebrated, the names of the waiters and waitresses who served them. A Dodge City native, I arrived in Wichita in 1997, and I never had a chance to step foot inside most of these iconic establishments. (Though I'm still kicking myself that I didn't visit Albert's before it closed in 2001 and didn't realize until years later what a mistake I'd made.)

Over the years, I'd occasionally write stories about readers' restaurant memories, and during my research, I'd become overwhelmed with a sense of wistful sadness and a desire to hop in a time machine and travel back just long enough to see these places for myself—to walk on the marble floors, to sit in the rattan chairs, to see the finely dressed people lining up outside for a seat, to watch as plates of fried chicken or liverwurst sandwiches were whisked to tables. *Wichita Eagle* restaurant writers of the past, including Diane, Fran and Kathleen Kelly, painted vivid pictures of these places with their words—words I soaked in while researching this book. But I would do anything to see them for myself. Now that I've spent the past year diving deeper into the history of these places and meeting the people or relatives of the people who started them, that longing is even more intense.

Before I started on this book, these iconic restaurants were like blank coloring book pages in my mind. As I researched each one and interviewed people who owned them or worked in them, the details appeared in vivid color. Sometimes I worry I'm over-romanticizing these places, but then I read another article from the archive or talk to someone who was lucky enough to have been a regular at one of these restaurants, and I realize that, nah, they really were that amazing. I'm proud and honored to have been asked to create a history of the Wichita restaurants that have meant so much to the city during its 151 years of existence.

I decided to approach this book in a chronological fashion, starting with a quick look at Wichita's first fifty years of restaurants and then traveling forward through the decades. That format helps illustrate how dining trends changed through the years and also reflects how Wichita grew. I was surprised, for example, how many times I had to type the phrase, "The restaurant was forced to move to make way for Kellogg expansion."

It was hard to choose which restaurants to include in the finished product, but ultimately, I did so by mentally (and sometimes physically) tallying up the number of times a restaurant was mentioned during my past reporting and polling or talked about on popular local Facebook pages like "If you grew up in wichita, ks, then you remember" and "Wichita history from my perspective."

I also showed my list to quite a few trusted local restaurant historians, who were eager to point out places I missed. Nevertheless, I'm sure I left out many that deserve to be included, but I'm confident that I got most of the big ones. (Maybe a volume two will be in order.)

Another question I struggled with was when to stop, and I settled on the 1980s. The most modern restaurant I profile in this book is the Old Town pioneer Pasta Mill, which was iconic in its day and has now been gone long enough to inspire passionate bouts of nostalgia.

Also, I decided to devote the bulk of the book to the iconic restaurants that are no longer operating. But as any student of Wichita restaurants knows, several of the city's most legendary restaurants are somehow still in business, and some have managed to keep operating for nearly 100 years. Two of those places—Livingston's Diner and Livingston's Cafe—can trace their roots back 111 years. Of course, these operational iconic restaurants—Old Mill Tasty Shop, NuWay, Savute's, Angelo's and so on—must be included in an account of Wichita's restaurant history, so I devoted a chapter to them, too.

Finally, I tried to keep this book mostly focused on restaurants that were started by and owned by locals, but I had to include a few chains. Pizza Hut and White Castle were no-brainers since they were started in Wichita. But chains like Grandy's, Steak and Ale, Chi Chi's and Shakey's Pizza Parlor were an undeniable part of Wichita's fabric during their time, and I decided they needed to be included.

I've always said that people who live outside of Wichita and assume that a mid-sized city in Kansas couldn't possibly have a great dining scene couldn't be more incorrect. Though we're missing some variety that big cities enjoy (and we're always a few years behind on the big dining trends), Wichita is the Lebanese food capital of the Midwest, thanks to the many immigrants from that country—including Latour's revered Antoine Toubia—who helped build our dining scene into what it is today.

Immigrants have also filled our city with amazing Vietnamese and Mexican fare, and it's never been difficult to find a good steak, a greasy burger or a unique serving of "Wich-Italian"-style pasta in this town. All of that is thanks to the generations of restaurant entrepreneurs who were brave enough to leave their home countries, risk their fortunes and work night and day just to feed the people who live here.

Their delicious work deserves to be remembered, and I hope I've done them justice in these pages.

PART I

WICHITA'S FIRST RESTAURANTS

1870-1915

Saloons, Chili Parlors and a Fred Harvey House

The earliest Wichita restaurants profiled in-depth in this book will be the Innes Tea Room, a luxurious place to see and be seen that opened in 1916 and later relocated to the top floor of the Innes Department Store, and T.J. Rice's Cafeteria, whose owner opened his first business downtown that same year.

But from the time Wichita was incorporated as a city in 1870, when its population was 689, until the Innes Tea Room opened forty-six years later, Wichita was filled with little restaurants, lunch counters and "refreshment stands," most of them operating on Douglas, Main, Market, Water and Lawrence Avenue, which today is known as Broadway.

Wichita's early growth was spurred by its location on the Chisholm Trail, and in the 1870s, cowboys like Wyatt Earp and Bat Masterson could be seen around town entertaining themselves in saloons and dance halls, especially in the rough-and-tumble Delano area. Visitors would often get their meals at boardinghouses and saloons, which served basic fare like meat, bread, potatoes and beans. In 1872, Wichita had fourteen saloons, but not all of them served food.

Wichita's earliest city directories list businesses by category, and they include sections for restaurants, bakeries, lunch counters and confectioneries. But the number of businesses serving food was nothing like it is today. The 1883 city directory, for example, lists just thirteen restaurants.

One of Wichita's earliest and most prominent restaurateurs was a portly, colorful man named Fritz Schnitzler (who later simplified the spelling of his

Fritz Snitzler was one of Wichita's earliest saloon owners and restaurateurs. His saloon is pictured in the center of this 1870s-era photo of a young Wichita. *Wichita–Sedgwick County Historical Museum.*

name to Snitzler). By 1876, he owned a big development at Douglas Avenue and Main Street commonly referred to as "Snitzville." It included a business called Apollo Saloon along with a hotel that housed a restaurant. A frequent character in early accounts of Wichita, Snitzler was a regular advertiser in newspapers, and in 1875, he bragged in the *Wichita Daily Eagle* that some days, he fed as many as seventy men dinner at a time. The ad read, "$100.00 Reward if anybody will beat Fritz Schnitzler on accommodations, at his restaurant, Boarding and Lodging."

In the 1877 Wichita directory, Snitzler was described as being "fully as liberal and jolly as he is heavy." The account went on: "Fritz knows how to run a Restaurant, and never allows his guest to go away dissatisfied. When you go to Wichita take your dinner there."

Among Wichita's other early eating establishments were places like the Arcade Restaurant on Douglas between Main and Water Streets, which was owned by Ed Loke. According to an 1878 announcement in the *Wichita Weekly Beacon*, "The quality and quantity of palatable food set before his guests is unsurpassed by any hotel or restaurant in this city."

Also in 1877, a "Mrs. Kemp" sold twenty-five-cent meals at all hours at her Eureka Restaurant, which was on Douglas Avenue between Fourth and Fifth Streets. And that same year, German immigrant F. Wilke opened

Cincinnati Bakery on Douglas south of Emporia. An ad that ran in the *Wichita Weekly Beacon* for several years described the business as "one of the neatest bakeries in the city. All kinds of bread, fresh cakes, pies, candies and eats, always on hand." It also sold, according to *Wichita's Daily Leader*, gingerbread, wedding cakes made to order and "ice cream for babies."

In 1879, W.P. Smith sold his restaurant on Main between Douglas and First to a Mrs. Hovey, and she had all manner of trouble for years to come. Reports published in local newspapers, for example, describe an incident in which a diner refused to pay for his breakfast, causing Mrs. Hovey to call the police, but not before the diner was overheard saying he intended to "beat Mrs. Hovey out of the bill." She made the paper again when a coal lamp exploded and damaged twenty-five dollars' worth of her clothing, then again when "Mrs. Hovey ejected a drunken fool from her restaurant this afternoon by force," as reported in an August edition of Wichita's *Daily Republican*.

By 1886, the Detroit Dining Parlor was open at 223 East Douglas. The Wichita–Sedgwick County Historical Museum has a photo of its owners and staff standing stone-faced out front. The restaurant was owned by Mrs. M.J.

The Detroit Dining Parlor operated in the mid-1880s at 223 East Douglas. *Wichita–Sedgwick County Historical Museum.*

HARRY KISTLER DEAD

Accidentally Shot Near Cheney Yesterday Morning.

WAS HELPING HIS DOG

Into the Buggy to Come Home From a Hunt.

A story about restaurant owner Harry Kistler's tragic death appeared in the December 1, 1899 edition of the *Wichita Eagle*.

Blackburn, who appeared to suffer fools about as patiently as Mrs. Hovey. In an 1887 help-wanted ad in the *Wichita Eagle*, she asks for two cooks, women preferred, and promises "good wages to the right party that can do first class work. No use for scrubs at any price."

The 1890s saw the continued success of longtime Wichita restaurateurs like George Puls, who ran a successful restaurant at 121 West Douglas that put out "the best dinner to be had in the city for the money," according to the *Wichita Opinion* in 1893. "His charge is only fifteen cents per meal and he never lets you go away hungry." Puls was still operating the restaurant with the help of his brothers, Herman and John, in 1911.

Also continuing his restaurant reign was Harry Kistler, who in 1893 was poised to open "one of the finest lunch rooms ever seen in this city" at 133 North Main. He'd been in the restaurant business for seven years at that point, having also run a lunchroom at 215 North Main as well as other restaurants with names like Red Front and Blue Front. In 1899, he died in a tragic accident when, at the end of a day of post-Thanksgiving hunting near Cheney, he was helping his dog into his buggy when the dog's paw accidentally pressed the trigger of Kistler's cocked gun and he was shot in the face. His widow vowed to continue their restaurant business, and by 1903, she was opening a new place of her own at 206 West Douglas.

City directories from the early 1900s list dozens of Wichita restaurants, many of them focusing on "short orders." Among them: Peoples' Restaurant at 346 North Main, Legal Tender Cafe at 509 East Douglas, Chesapeake Cafe at 115 East Douglas and Delmonico Cafe at 115 South Lawrence. The early 1900s also saw the opening of a slew of chili parlors, which specialized in chili, tamales and ice cream and also often sold cigars. They all operated on or near Douglas Avenue and had names like Ed Ceros Place, H.L. Dewing's Chili Parlor, H.E. Diggs' Chili Parlor, John Seal's Chili Parlor and The Up-To-Date Chili and Tamale Parlor.

Meanwhile, tearooms, cafeterias and chop suey restaurants run by a new wave of Chinese immigrants were gaining traction across the United States, and they were on their way to Wichita.

WICHITA GETS A HARVEY HOUSE

Wichita's dining scene took a big step forward in 1914, when a restaurant company founded by Fred Harvey—who is credited with creating the country's first restaurant chain—opened a dining room in the brand-new Union Station train terminal.

Harvey, who died in 1901, had worked in the restaurant business in New York, and he frequently traveled by train. Frustrated by the difficulty train passengers experienced trying to get a decent meal, in the mid-1870s, he approached the Santa Fe Railway with a proposal to open eating houses at all of its train stops. He started with a twenty-seat lunchroom at the railway's train station in Topeka, then expanded into Florence, Newton, Hutchison and Dodge City. His "Harvey Girls"—the waitresses he trained to courteously and quickly feed passengers coming in and out of the train stations—became famous nationwide. Their uniforms were long black dresses covered with white aprons, and they lived by a strict Harvey code of conduct that included a curfew. That attention to detail also was reflected in the dining rooms themselves, which used high-end dishes, linens and

The new Union Station train terminal opened in 1914 with a Fred Harvey Eating House inside. *Wichita–Sedgwick County Historical Museum.*

19

furniture. The Fred Harvey chain quickly expanded and would eventually include not only train station eating rooms but also hotel restaurants and dining cars. At the peak of the Harvey company's success, it was operating eighty-four eating houses.

In 1913, Wichita broke ground on the new Union Station, part of a $2.5 million railroad-funded project that included elevating the tracks at Kellogg, Douglas, First and Second Streets. The Harvey company won the bid to put a restaurant in the station, which resulted in much excitement locally, as the chain's reputation preceded it. A story in an April 1913 issue of the *Wichita Beacon* said that the dining room would accommodate seventy diners and would be "finished in Flemish style, with antique chairs and decorations." The finished product featured a semicircular marble lunch counter and more marble-topped tables positioned throughout.

Harvey's family ran the company after his death and continued operating it until 1968, when it was sold to a hospitality company called Amfac Inc. Wichita's Harvey Eating House lasted until 1935, when the company closed it and cut back to a soda fountain with lunch offerings. But just as it had in many other cities across the country, the Harvey House brand made its mark on Wichita.

1916-1929

Tearooms, Cafeterias and the Rise of the Chop Suey Palace

INNES TEA ROOM (1916)

If you were a lady who lunched, if you had out-of-town visitors to impress, if you wanted to don your best dress and your white gloves, to see and be seen while nibbling on tiny tea sandwiches, the Innes Tea Room was where you went in early Wichita.

Even today, many Wichitans who recall dining at the Innes Tea Room, which initially opened in 1916, describe it with reverence and remember it as a place that symbolized the magic of a simpler yet more formal time.

The tearoom first opened on Friday, May 5, 1916, in an annex directly north of the Innes Dry Goods Company, which at the time was at Douglas and Broadway and sold everything from cosmetics to furs to refrigerators. The new tearoom occupied a 75-by-140-foot second-floor space and cost $5,000 to install. Shoppers accessed it via a bridge that connected the two buildings.

In its early years, the tearoom featured white tablecloths and "Austrian puff curtains in buff with draperies of burnt orange velvet," according to a 1919 edition of the *Wichita Beacon*, and it was the place to dine if you were somebody. The social pages of the *Wichita Daily Eagle* and *Wichita Beacon* were filled with announcements of dinners put on there by people entertaining visitors from out of town, by gracious hostesses hoping to surprise members of their reading circles, by fraternity and sorority groups with important

The Innes Tea Room operated on the sixth floor of the Innes Department Store. *William Sloan Jr.*

business to discuss or by couples wanting to dine before retiring to a private home to dance in the New Year.

An ad published in the *Wichita Beacon* days after the new tearoom's opening described the menu, which offered meals ranging from thirty-five to seventy-five cents, in tempting terminology: "There now comes a new realization of the joy in eating what you like—pies that 'melt in your mouth'—meats that 'make one's palate sing'—salads with zest that fully answers the call of a lusty appetite—vegetables that bring all the blessings nature stored in them and such coffee as only an 'inspired' cook can make."

People would dine at the Innes Tea Room before taking in a performance at one of many theaters and entertainment venues within walking distance. A handily illustrated ad printed in 1922 touts that the tearoom is "in the heart of the theater district" and just across the street from the Miller Theatre, four hundred feet north of the Orpheum Theatre and just around the corner from the Wichita Theatre.

The tearoom moved in 1927 to the top floor of the department store's new six-story building. The new space had seating for four hundred in the main dining room, which was appointed with Spanish-style décor, plus four private dining rooms. There was also a separate Men's Private Grill, which was decorated "in the Italian manner," according to a 1928 write-up in *Wichita This Week*, where men would enjoy cigars while the ladies had their meals.

An early menu lists several simple dishes that customers could enjoy, including breaded veal cutlets with Russian beets and spiced crab apple, or tuna fish croquettes with celery and olive sauce, scalloped potatoes and sliced tomatoes. Hot rolls and biscuits were always available, and diners would finish with a slice of rum cream pie.

Its early years predated the common use of air conditioning, and customers in 1923 were lured by advertisements promising "seventeen fans to keep you cool while taking lunch" and ice-cold watermelon available for ten cents a slice. When the tearoom installed air conditioning in 1934, it was a momentous occasion.

Wichita's dining hot spot was not immune to the effects of World War II, and an ad printed in local newspapers in August 1943 announced that it, too, had to bend to food rationing and could serve only 650 lunches and 400 dinners a day.

"The Innes Tea Room and the housewife have a common problem—making the most of the foods available. But add to our problem the fact that more people are dining out, satisfactory help is getting scarcer every day, many eating places have closed because of these problems, and you can readily see what we are up against," the ad read.

The Innes Department Store was sold to Younker Brothers of Des Moines in 1951, and four years later, it sold to R.H. Macy and Co. The tearoom lasted until 1973, and Macy's lasted until 1986, when Dillard's bought it out. The store closed for good in 1988 and eventually became a state office building. In 2017, it was sold to local developer Sudha Tokala, who says she plans to turn it into a medical and trade school complex.

But many current Wichitans still fondly recall going to the tearoom to see fashion shows, and they remember dressing up and putting on white gloves. Over the years since it closed, many fundraising events have taken place where organizers draw crowds by re-creating the look, feel and menu of the Innes Tea Room.

T.J. RICE'S CAFETERIA (1916)

One of Wichita's earliest and most self-promoting restaurateurs was T.J. Rice, but his fortunes burned bright and then burned out. Rice, who had spent many years in the restaurant business, moved to Wichita from

In order to enjoy such a wonderful celebration
pure and wholesome food is the first essential

Obtainable at

T. J. Rice's Cafeteria
"Quality"

114-16 S. Lawrence Ave.   Opposite Princess Theatre

Noon   —— OPEN ——   Evening
11:00 to 2:00   5:00 to 7:30

T.J. Rice's Cafeteria was one of Wichita's premier restaurants when it opened in the early 1900s. This ad appeared in the *Wichita Eagle* on October 3, 1920.

Hutchinson in 1916 and opened a cafeteria at 125 North Market, which he sold after about six months. In 1918, he opened another café at 138 North Market, and it proved so successful that he soon needed a larger space, which he found at 114–116 South Lawrence Avenue, which today is Broadway. He called the new business T.J. Rice's Cafeteria, and it was described by the *Wichita Beacon* as being the largest cafeteria in Kansas, with a dining room that was fifty by ninety feet and served two meals a day—one at noon and one in the evening. It fed 1,000 to 1,200 people each day, the paper said, and Rice employed 30 people with a weekly payroll that totaled $450. An advertisement that ran in the *Wichita Eagle* in

1920 included a photo of the interior, which was filled with wooden dining chairs pushed up against long tables situated under a tin ceiling fitted with several ceiling fans.

Rice developed a habit of taking out ads in the papers to speak directly to his customers about the superiority of his cafeteria and to explain to them how it worked. In an announcement published in the *Wichita Beacon* in May 1918, he told his customers that although he was sure they were "a little provoked" to find him gone from his old location, they just needed to find the new one. When they arrived, he said, they should enter through the north door, walk down the north wall to the meat table and proceed across to the vegetables, salads and fruit. Before customers left, he told them in the ad, they'd get a check for their meal. "Retain it and pay my son, Fay, as you leave the building." That same ad promised customers that everything they'd loved about his North Market restaurant could be found at the new one.

"The first things I transported were the women cooks," the ad said. "Without them I could not run a cafeteria successfully. I attribute my success in the business to my wonderful cooks. They are the best in the world. I wouldn't have any other kind and no one can take them away from me— they have been with me too long."

Rice's cooks were a major point of pride. A few months later, he took out another ad in the *Wichita Eagle* to extol their virtues: "It has been quite a long time since I have talked with *Eagle* readers about my women cooks and the wholesome healthy food they cook. In fact we have been so busy down at this Cafeteria that we have had no time to talk with anyone except ourselves and what we will prepare to tickle the palates of our friends."

In August 1918, Rice's cashier son, Fay, started his own business called Rice's Cafe at 118 West Douglas. But two years later, both father and son were bankrupt. T.J. Rice filed a voluntary petition of bankruptcy in December 1920, listing his liabilities at $11,000 and his assets as not more than $8,000. A few days later, Fay filed his own bankruptcy petition, listing his father as his largest creditor.

A story about the bankruptcy that appeared in the December 2, 1920 issue of the *Wichita Beacon* informed readers of the turn of events: "Because of the large volume of patronage at the Rice Cafeteria and the satisfaction it rendered to the public, the bankruptcy proceedings are attracting more than ordinary attention," the article read. "This petition comes to a surprise to the public altho it has been rumored among the circle of creditors for some time.

T.J.'s friend George R. Basset was appointed receiver of Rice's Cafeteria and put in charge, though he retained T.J. Rice as manager. Rice's Cafe, though, closed, and in 1921, it was purchased by Paul Fotopolous of Newton and reopened as Sunflower Restaurant.

The last time Rice's Cafeteria is mentioned in the papers is 1921, and a business college soon took over the space.

WHITE CASTLE (1916)

Today, the White Castle chain sells its signature square-shaped sliders in 375 restaurants across fourteen states. And even though Kansas isn't one of them, Wichitans know that White Castle got its start there and that its legacy lingered for decades after it left.

It all began in 1916, when Walt Anderson opened a five-stool stand on East Douglas and offered pressed-beef sandwiches—widely believed to be among the first burgers ever sold. He served his burgers on dinner rolls to soak up the grease and topped them with onions and pickles. Within two years, he opened another stand with proceeds from his popular venture, and by 1920, he had four hamburger stands. That's when he partnered with Edgar Waldo "Billy" Ingram, a well-known insurance and real estate man who was Anderson's friend and was looking for a side business.

The two agreed to call their hamburger stands White Castle, and they designed buildings that looked somewhat like tiny castles. The first official White Castle opened in 1921 at 201 North Main Street and sold burgers by the sack for five cents apiece.

White Castle became more popular over the next decade and opened several stands around Wichita at addresses like 1247 East Douglas, 215 East William, 112 South St. Francis, 146 North Emporia, 115 East Second and 119 South Water. In the 1930s, the owners started opening their restaurants in "modern" enameled metal buildings. Then, the chain began spreading outside of Wichita. Anderson led the venture until 1934, when the headquarters moved to Columbus, Ohio. He retired, leaving Ingram in charge. At the time, there were 123 White Castles operating in sixteen cities. The last White Castle hamburger stand in Wichita closed in 1938, and

Above: White Castle opened in Wichita in 1916. *White Castle.*

Opposite: Billy Ingram was the founder of White Castle. *White Castle.*

longtime manager A.J. "Jimmie" King bought 3 of them, renaming them Kings-X and starting a local empire of his own.

But Wichita never forgot White Castle, and residents still bemoan the unfairness of the fact that the city where it all started can get White Castle burgers only in boxes in grocery store freezer sections.

In 2011, when the chain was celebrating its ninetieth birthday, it put on a special homecoming event in the Dillons grocery store parking lot at Central Avenue and Rock Road in Wichita. The chain wanted to acknowledge the city where it was born, and for two hours one May afternoon, it grilled up White Castle burgers and sold them to Wichitans for ninety cents apiece. Thousands turned out to get their sliders, which over the years have been referred to as "gut bombs" and "belly busters." The wait for a burger was an hour and a half at some points, leaving one attendee to describe the event to the *Wichita Eagle* as "a mess of humanity and beef."

Today, the nearest White Castle to Wichita is 320 miles away in Columbia, Missouri.

PAN-AMERICAN CAFE (1917)

In 1920, Wichita was home to only about eighteen Chinese people, and they were all men. Nearly all of them worked at Pan-American Cafe, a long, skinny restaurant at 150 North Market that opened in 1917. The restaurant specialized in chop suey, a stir-fry dish that has no roots in China, and other Americanized versions of Chinese dishes that Wichita palates could tolerate.

In the early days, Pan-American Cafe was run by five young immigrants who had come to America, some using false papers and leaving their wives and children behind in China. They lived in tiny rooms above the café. Among the early operators of the restaurant was the congenial host, King Mar, who was the face of the restaurant until the day it closed in 1969. Jimmy Wong was the head chef, and Mar Tung Jing also helped run the restaurant, which featured a lunch counter with stools and a case filled with cigars for sale at the entrance. Though King Mar came to the United States in 1914, his wife was not able to join him until 1956. It was a similar story for King's partner, Mar Tung Jing, who left his wife and three-month-old son in China to move to the United States in 1922. She was not able to join him until after World War II.

The restaurant was known for its barbecued pork, which was a specialty of Mar Tung Jing. But Chinese food made up only about a third of the menu. The rest was filled with American dishes like tomato soup and roast turkey.

Left: The Pan-American Cafe opened at 150 North Market in 1917. *Edward Wong*.

Below: The Pan-American Cafe was a stylish place for oil and cattle men to hold business meetings. *Edward Wong*.

It was a stylish place for oil and cattle men to hold business meetings, remembered Ed Wong, the grandson of Mar Tung Jing. The restaurant was so popular that it often packed in three hundred people over lunch, and for some time, it was open twenty-four hours a day to meet the demand.

Ed's father, Wayne, was also a restaurateur who had worked at T-Bone Supper Club and owned Georgie Porgie Pancake Shop. Ed went on to become a local Long John Silver's franchisee and to open Wichita's Spaghetti Jack's restaurants.

Since there were no Chinese women in Wichita in the restaurant's early days, local women were hired as servers. The cooks could not read English, though, according to early accounts of the restaurant, so the waitresses had to shout out the orders. More authentic ingredients were hard to get in Wichita, and the Pan-American staff caused a big hubbub in 1921 when a shipment of duck feet from Chicago was intercepted by freight handlers, whose attention was attracted by "a nauseous odor which apparently emanated from one of the packages," according to the *Wichita Eagle*. The weighing inspector decided that narcotics, most likely opium, were hidden in the package. The café owners and their lawyer came back days later with an impassioned defense of their café.

When the Pan-American Cafe closed in June 1969, the *Wichita Eagle* estimated that it was the oldest restaurant in the state that had operated under the same management. On closing day, a serving of chow mein cost eighty cents. Interviewed by the *Eagle* on the eve of the restaurant's closing, King Mar said that Pan-American Cafe had gotten old and wages were too high. Remodeling would cost too much, so the partners decided to retire.

Said the *Eagle* article, "Mar, interviewed on Friday, admitted, 'I will miss all my customers,' but there was a happy grin on his almost youthful face when he said he was not sad to retire."

WOLF'S CAFETERIA (1919)

Ernest Wolf was born in Bern, Switzerland, and his father died when Ernest was just five years old. As a boy, he worked for a bakery, so when he and his brother relocated to Kansas in 1887, lured by his maternal uncle who had started an Indian trade post in Wichita, Ernest looked for another bakery job.

He found one at Bissantz Bakery, which had operated since 1894 at 416 East Douglas. He met and fell for his boss's niece Emelie Bissantz, and his

Wolf's Cafeteria was torn down to make way for Century II parking. *Stephen Wolf.*

future in the bakery business was cemented. In 1898, Ernest bought a bakery at 111 South Main, which he ran for twenty years, selling honey bread, rolls, cakes and pastries. In 1901, he married Emelie, and they had a son, Arthur.

Eventually, Ernest was ready to expand his business. He'd been to California and witnessed a new concept called a "cafeteria," where customers could go down a line and get anything they wanted. He liked it, and in 1919, he partnered with Charles O. Parrott to open a new cafeteria that would become a central Wichita dining and meeting place for the next four decades.

The cafeteria was at 115–117 South Main—just north of the old downtown library and just south of the Century Plaza building at Douglas and Main—where today there's a Century II parking lot with metered spaces. On opening day, the cafeteria could seat 240. It featured white tables with wooden chairs, where diners in hats and bonnets would sit after going through the line and choosing from à la carte meats, vegetables and desserts that would be served to them by employees sporting white paper hats.

Wolf and Parrott expanded the cafeteria two years later, taking over a shop space to the south and enlarging their footprint to nearly eleven thousand square feet. By then, the cafeteria had an upstairs mezzanine level for meetings and a horseshoe-shaped counter at the front filled with jars of colorful candy sticks. Things were going so well that the same year, 1921, they opened a branch cafeteria at 125 North Market in a space that had previously been occupied by Home Cafeteria.

An article from that year's *Wichita Eagle* declared the main cafeteria, at the time called Wolf & Parrott's, "the largest in the southwest and larger than any cafeteria in Kansas City." Downtown workers were drawn to the restaurant because of its large selection, its low prices and the fact that, because food was served cafeteria style, they didn't need to tip. The *Wichita*

Wolf's Cafeteria was once one of Wichita's most popular dining destinations. *Stephen Wolf.*

People could choose whatever they wanted from the cafeteria line at Wolf's Cafeteria. *Stephen Wolf.*

Eagle said in August 1921 that the business was serving 1,600 a day on Main Street and another 550 a day on Market.

"One element contributing to the success of this firm is a study of the comfort of patrons," the article read. "Costly ventilation systems have been installed in both cafeterias." By 1922, the cafeteria was being enthusiastically recommended on the *Eagle*'s society page by Dolly Varden in a column called Dolly Varden Goes Shopping.

"A friend of mine remarked the other day as we were standing at the corner of Main and Douglas, 'Where are all the people going, is there a fire or something.'" Varden wrote, "I told her that it was people going to Wolf & Parrott's Cafeteria for lunch, and as a woman's curiosity has to be satisfied, we followed the crowd to Wolf & Parrott's and were well repaid, and now we know why the people of Wichita are constantly streaming in and out of Wolf & Parrott's."

Among the dishes diners could enjoy at the cafeteria were "crisp salads, cool desserts," fried chicken and delicacies like baked goose and mincemeat pies at Thanksgiving and Christmastime. A live orchestra frequently entertained diners in the evening, and Wichitans remember that Ernest would frequently be there wearing his white restaurant coat with his name embroidered on the front.

Ernest brought his son, Arthur, into the business in 1925, and in 1928, they bought Parrott out. The restaurant was known after that as Wolf's Cafeteria. Father and son remodeled the place in 1930, expanding their dining capacity to five hundred. In 1936, they added a banquet room where many a company Christmas party took place for years to come.

Ernest Wolf retired in 1956 at the age of eighty-three, leaving the business to his son, Arthur. He died three years later. Arthur's son, Stephen, who made his career in the theater business, remembered that when his father found out the business would have to move as part of Wichita's urban renewal program, he asked Stephen if he wanted to take it over.

But Stephen, who had worked in the cafeteria from boyhood washing dishes, had other ideas. He'd gone to college and wanted to strike out on his own. His father decided to close the store rather than relocate it. In the following years, cafeteria concepts like Forum and Furr's started expanding and growing in popularity, and Stephen sometimes wondered if he'd made the wrong decision. But the lessons his grandfather and father taught him about building a business and expanding it served him well in life, he said. And even though he chose a different entrepreneurial path, he can still hear his father's advice in his ears: "Bakery is the business to be in. People will always want bread."

HOLLY CAFE (1926)

Pan-American Cafe may have been the earliest influential Chinese restaurant in Wichita, but it wasn't the only one. A similar restaurant called Holly Cafe also had its fair share of customers. It opened at 105 West Douglas in 1926, the first year it is mentioned in any Wichita publications. In 1928, it relocated to 119 West Douglas, where records indicate it operated until it closed in the 1960s to make way for the construction of Century II and the Wichita Public Library.

Among its early owners was Gook Poy Mar, who at age twelve was brought from China to the United States by an aunt and uncle. He went to work for Sam Mardock, another Chinese immigrant, who started a successful restaurant in Tyler, Texas, called Cottonbelt. Poy learned the restaurant business at Cottonbelt, and in the 1920s, Poy relocated to Wichita, where the Pan-American Cafe was already thriving, and helped open Holly Cafe.

Douglas Avenue, Looking East, Wichita, Kansas

A postcard shows Douglas Avenue looking east in the 1930s. Holly Cafe's sign can be seen at lower right. *Tanner McFall Inc.*

The menu was almost identical to the one at Cottonbelt and offered a mix of Chinese and American dishes, including chop suey and egg foo young as well as sirloin beef tips and mashed potatoes.

An advertisement that ran in local publications in the late 1920s boasted that Holly Cafe served "chop suey put up to take home" as well as "special breakfasts," "good lunch" for thirty-five cents and "excellent Sunday dinner." Just a block from the Broadview Hotel, Holly Cafe would often draw customers who were staying there, and it along with Pan-American Cafe was popular with the small but growing Chinese community.

"They were kind of like the heartbeat of the city from a Chinese perspective," said Poy's grandson Larry Mark Wong. "You could get Chinese food or you could get American food." Larry Mark Wong noted

OPEN DAY AND NIGHT
"Right in the Heart of Town"
SPECIAL BREAKFASTS
GOOD LUNCH 35c
Excellent Sunday Dinner

HOLLY CAFE
105 WEST DOUGLAS
Chop Suey Put Up To Take
Home
Specialists in all Kinds of
Chinese Dishes
D7485   Phones   M1517

An advertisement for Holly Cafe that ran in a 1928 edition of *Wichita This Week*.

he still has a few memories from Holly Cafe and can picture his grandfather cooking in the kitchen.

Holly Cafe and Pan-American Cafe were especially influential in the growth of early Wichita, he said. Though many Chinese restaurants popped up in Wichita in the 1920s and 1930s—King Fong Cafe, Mandarin Inn, Nanking Cafe and Air Capital Cafe among them—only Pan-American, Holly and Fairland Cafes made it to the end of the 1930s. The group of men who founded Pan-American Cafe and Holly Cafe were all distantly related and had roots in the same village in China. Their descendants would go on to open a long list of other restaurants, liquor stores and businesses in early Wichita.

After Holly Cafe closed, Poy and his son, also named Larry Wong, went on to open South City Restaurant at 1714 Northern in Wichita. It was open from 1967 until Larry Sr. and his wife, Jane, closed it in 2004. Its menu was virtually the same as the Chinese/American menu at Holly Cafe and included both chow mein and sirloin beef tips.

1930-1939

Home-Style Cooking Diners and White Castle's Departure

VALENTINE DINERS (1930s)

An account of Wichita's restaurant history wouldn't be complete without the inclusion of businessman Arthur Valentine, owner of Valentine Manufacturing Inc. The tiny prefab metal buildings his company constructed from the 1930s to the 1970s were used to house restaurants and other businesses across the country, and several are still in operation. In Wichita, Grinder Man and Sport Burger both operate in old Valentine diners.

The story starts in 1920, when Valentine, who was born in Illinois, moved to Kansas with his wife and started his own chain of lunchrooms. His first one was in the small Kansas town of Hazelton, and he soon expanded his business, opening restaurants in both Wichita and Hutchinson. His little chain was known as the Valentine Lunch System.

At the same time, the Ablah Company in Wichita got into manufacturing portable lunchrooms, which included stainless-steel lunch counters and bar stool seating. The lunchrooms were big enough for eight to ten diners and small enough that two people could operate them, giving people with big dreams but small fortunes a way to get into business for themselves. The Ablah Company sold one of its buildings to Valentine, who opened it as Shamrock Lunch in Hutchinson.

Before long, Valentine was working for Ablah as a salesman while he continued to operate his own restaurants. When owners of the Ablah Company decided they wanted out of the lunchroom business in the late 1930s, Valentine took it over. He struggled during World War II, when materials were scarce, but once the war ended, the business took off. He founded Valentine Industries in 1945, followed two years later by Valentine Manufacturing Inc. Even though most prefab diner manufacturers were on the East Coast, Valentine thrived. Though he died in 1954, his company is said to have produced more than two thousand Valentine diner units between 1938 and 1971. Most were turned into restaurants, but after Prohibition, the company also sold its prefab buildings to people wanting to open liquor stores.

After Valentine died, his company was sold, and it was out of business by the mid-1970s, when interest in the buildings waned. But the legacy lives on.

In addition to the two still-operating Valentine diners in Wichita, two other high-profile Valentines are sitting vacant: the Dyne Quik building at 1202 North Broadway, which first opened in 1959 but has been empty since 2015, and Brint's Diner at 4834 East Lincoln, whose most recent owner closed it in April 2021. Several other Valentine Diners that once operated in Wichita have been removed or relocated. But functional Valentine diners are located in cities all over Kansas and in states like Arizona, Colorado and Indiana.

POLAR BEAR (1930)

In 1966, Seth Wright was known as "Chicken Man." He was preparing to open the first of what he hoped would become a chain of Dixie Fried Chicken restaurants that year, and he allowed the *Wichita Beacon* to come watch his magic butchering skills. A caption that ran alongside a photo of Wright grasping a foot-long knife as he prepared to splay a chicken read: "When he's through, there will be 10 pieces."

According to the article, Wright had moved to Wichita in 1927, and a few years later, he bought a small drive-in for $350. The drive-in, which he called Polar Bear, was at 4729 East Central, and it opened in 1930. A photo from the Wichita–Sedgwick County Historical Museum, taken in 1938, is an eye-catcher and shows a little hut with artificial snowcaps on the roof and polar bear statues standing guard at either side of the front door. A menu posted outside offers root beer for five cents, a sundae or malt for fifteen cents and a "polar whip" or dish of frozen custard for a dime. According to a caption on the photo, the shop sat diagonally on the southwest corner of Central and Oliver.

Above: Polar Bear originally opened as a tiny custard stand on the corner of Central and Oliver in 1930. *Wichita–Sedgwick County Historical Museum.*

Right: This postcard shows the Polar Bear restaurant, which operated at Central and Oliver. The back of the postcard promises "rough and ready chicken. Fried rough— ready to eat." *Nationwide Advertising Specialty Co., Tyler, Texas.*

Polar Bear

Central and Oliver   Wichita 8, Kansas

View of Main Dining Room

In 1939, Wright expanded with a second Polar Bear Frozen Custard shop at Kellogg and Hydraulic, and at some point—though records aren't clear about exactly when—he added a five-hundred-seat Polar Bear restaurant on the Central and Oliver lot. An advertisement in a 1949 publication called *Downtown Wichita* announces the restaurant's grand opening and promises "air conditioned luxury," "competent, experienced, courteous service at amazing speed," "Southern fried chicken…done to a perfect turn" and "pastry from our own kitchen to delight you." Mrs. (Ada) Whitcomb, the ad said, would be entertaining at the organ, and the restaurant would also have a private party room.

An old postcard shows what the restaurant looked like: the exterior was brick and had a large sign featuring the image of a polar bear. The interior was filled with lush plants, rows of red-and-tan booths, light pink walls and gold drapes. The back of the postcard says that the restaurant served "Rough and Ready Chicken, Fried Rough, Ready to Eat," plus "All kinds of steaks served piping hot" and "Delicious Frozen Custard." The restaurant was open from 11:00 a.m. to 11:00 p.m. seven days a week. It appears to have later also operated at both 2602 South Oliver and at 2955 South Hillside.

Fast-forward to 1966, and Wright shared his plans with the *Wichita Eagle* to establish worldwide fried chicken dominance. His first Dixie Fried Chicken restaurant would be at 3255 East Harry, and he planned four more for Wichita. After that, he planned to open Dixie restaurants "all over the world." He'd already placed an ad in a Chicago-based restaurant magazine, he said, and received more than four thousand inquiries from interested parties in all fifty states.

Wright opened the East Harry restaurant, but in September 1967—a little more than a year after he announced his plans in the *Wichita Eagle*—he died at age seventy-two. Mentions of the Dixie Fried Chicken restaurant on Harry disappear after October 1968. Just two years before, a hopeful Wright had told the *Wichita Eagle*, "I hate the thought of going into retirement and taking all these secrets with me. I have learned that there are 1,001 ways to enter the chicken dinner business and fail but only one way to enter this business with small capital and succeed."

As of this writing, a liquor store called Central Market Wine & Spirits operates in the old Polar Bear site at Central and Oliver. Its owner restored the building's brick exterior, and it looks more like the former restaurant than it has in years. Photos of the Polar Bear restaurant and the frozen custard stand that preceded it hang in the liquor store's entrance.

GARVIE'S RESTAURANT (1932)

Another name that figures prominently into Wichita restaurant lore is Annamae Garvie, a Kansas State University graduate and former cafeteria supervisor for Wichita public schools who in 1932 partnered with George Droll and his sister to open a new downtown restaurant. It was called Droll's Restaurant, and it served home-style cooking out of a building at 117 North Broadway, right next door to the Miller Theatre.

After seven years in business, Garvie bought out her partner, who leased a different building at Central and Hillside (later known as Droll's English Grill). Garvie, meanwhile, changed the name of her place to Garvie's Restaurant. Over the next four decades, she would become one of Wichita's most respected restaurant owners running one of Wichita's most popular restaurants. When Garvie's Restaurant closed in 1970, Wichitans were bereft. Downtown workers, who had long lauded Garvie's affordable and tasty fare, said they couldn't imagine where else they would eat.

Annamae Garvie personally oversaw her popular Garvie's Restaurant at 117 North Broadway until it closed in 1970. *From the* Wichita Eagle.

41

Wichita Eagle columnist Don Granger wrote in a nostalgic column published in 1976: "The food tasted like home cooking—often better than some I've known. This created dozens (perhaps hundreds) of regular customers and this made the restaurant into a special place where there always was room at a table or booth to sit with friends and gossip."

When the restaurant first opened, it served twenty-five-cent plates that came with a meat, vegetable, salad, roll and a drink. For thirty-five cents, customers could get a grilled steak with fries over the lunch hour, but the plate went up to forty-five cents in the evening.

Garvie was an exacting boss who personally inspected the food going out to her customers. "Miss Garvie was always concerned about the way the plate looked as well as how food tasted," remembered one employee interviewed by the *Wichita Eagle*.

Carol Webb, a Wichitan who worked at Garvie's as a teenager in the mid-1950s, remembered that the staff was loyal to Garvie, and there wasn't much waitress turnover. Almost as well known as Garvie herself was Ada Stutzman, her longtime manager, who knew the faces of the restaurant's regulars and could remember where they wanted to sit and what they wanted to eat.

Webb recalled that, during her time, the restaurant opened at 11:00 a.m. and a line of people would always be outside waiting to enter. When they came in, they could choose a seat on the main floor or sit in the balcony, where they could look over the railing and watch the activity below.

Once they got to the head of the line, they could order the day's special and then pass by a smorgasbord, where they could choose salads and desserts. Then, after 1:00 p.m., the fountain would be open and people could order sandwiches, desserts or ice cream on the first floor. The dinner hour started at 5:00 p.m. and ran until 8:00 p.m., when waitresses would take orders at the tables. The dinner menu changed each day and included options like baked halibut, Salisbury steak and baked steak, though pan-fried chicken and T-bone steaks were always available.

Garvie was also known for a long list of other dishes that were popular at the time, things like ham loaf with horseradish sauce, hamburger and spaghetti, peaches and cottage cheese, lima bean salad, goose liver sandwiches, spoon bread, peas served with Spanish peanuts and devil's food cake. During World War II, Garvie was known to send that devil's food cake to employees who had gone overseas.

"Everything was done the old-fashioned way," Webb said. "The chicken was pan-fried, not deep-fried; the pies, cakes and rolls were made on site by women who came to work in the wee hours. I wish there was a restaurant now that had such good food."

In 1969, the Fourth National Bank bought the Miller Theatre building and property and offered to let Garvie, whose lease was up, keep the restaurant space on a temporary basis until she decided to close. Instead, she opted to retire. The bank razed the building in 1972 and a few years later built a parking garage on the site. Annamae Garvie died in 1983 at age eighty-seven.

CONTINENTAL GRILL (1936)

The Continental Grill chain of restaurants was popular in Wichita in the 1940s and 1950s, but the most well known operated at 1220 West Douglas. Harold Durant—who had learned his trade working for Fred Harvey's famous Harvey House chain of restaurants in the 1920s—opened the first Continental Grill at the corner of Central and Hillside in 1936, and one of his specialties was a twenty-five-cent chicken fried steak dinner. He went on to open ten restaurants before selling his chain in the late 1960s. Among the Wichita addresses Continental Grill restaurants called home over the years were 3012 East Douglas, 608 North Broadway, 1716 East Douglas and 7411 East Kellogg.

But the restaurant that still lives in the memory of many Wichitans was the one on West Douglas, which opened in 1955 and served as the west-side turnaround spot for teens "dragging Douglas." It was also the first restaurant in Kansas to offer electronic ordering.

"It was the place to see your friends," Harold Durant's son, Warren, told the *Wichita Eagle* in 1994. "If there were no parking spaces, at least you could see who was there when you drove through on your way to the Town and Country Drive-In at Pawnee and Hillside, then back to the Continental again." Another popular turnaround spot for Douglas draggers was Sandy's at Douglas and Grove. Some went as far as the Big Bun at Central and Oliver.

By the mid-1960s, though, Harold Durant was fed up with the teenagers who frequented his parking lot on West Douglas. He closed the drive-in portion in 1965, citing "rowdyism and misconduct" by local teens. By the late 1960s, he was trying to draw families in with Monday night "family buffets," a buffet breakfast on Sundays and an organ player. One of the restaurant's ads in the *Wichita Beacon* read: "Make Sunday a holiday for mother, too. Be thrifty. Go Continental."

Harold Durant died in 1989 at age eighty-four.

FAIRLAND CAFE (1938)

For decades, Wichitans with a hankering for chop suey at 3:00 a.m. could get it at Fairland Cafe, a Chinese restaurant at 116 South Broadway that operated just across the street from the Innes Department Store and never closed.

The restaurant was founded in the early 1900s by Chinese immigrants and originally called King Fong. A few years later, the space became a restaurant called Mandarin. Then, in 1938, Sai Young, a former owner of Holly Cafe at 105 West Douglas, along with a group of partners, bought the restaurant. They changed its name to Fairland Cafe.

Young's son, Chuck Mar, moved to Wichita in 1935 and worked alongside his father in his various restaurant jobs. Mar became the owner of Fairland Cafe in 1972, running it until its final day in February 1980.

The restaurant's heyday was in the war years, the 1930s and 1940s, when downtown Wichita was a hub of activity and the restaurant was always packed. The restaurant boasted a recognizable pagoda-shaped neon sign that promised chop suey could be found inside. It was known for its inexpensive lunch special: a heaping plate of chow mein, an egg roll, fried rice and two slices of Wonder brand rye bread. When the restaurant closed in 1980, the special still cost $1.75. The restaurant also served a large selection of American fare, and customers loved the chicken fried steak, haddock and liver and onions.

With its low prices and long hours, Fairland Cafe attracted working people, and it also drew a few celebrities. Its most famous visitor might have been John F. Kennedy, who made a stop in Wichita during his 1960 presidential campaign. He showed up sometime after midnight, the story went. He ate breakfast and played pinball on the machine that sat near a jukebox at the front of the restaurant.

Another, less savory character who frequented the restaurant was George Poulos, a local tough guy and convicted arsonist who was well known in Wichita and who died in 2010. He haunted the restaurant during its late-night and overnight hours, remembered Mar's son and daughter.

People who entered Fairland Cafe from the back would have to pass through the kitchen to get to the dining room, which had a single strip of neon light fixtures in the ceiling and a coat rack at each table.

In 1979, when oilman Jack Slawson bought the building on South Broadway that held the café, it was the only twenty-four-hour restaurant left downtown. Shortly after the purchase, owner Mar announced his plans to retire. After decades of running a twenty-four-hour restaurant, he told a

John F. Kennedy visited the twenty-four-hour Fairland Cafe at 116 South Broadway while traveling for his 1960 presidential campaign. *Wichita–Sedgwick County Historical Museum.*

reporter from the *Wichita Eagle*, he needed to rest. Plus, he noted, downtown wasn't like it used to be. No one was ever there after 6:00 p.m. anymore.

"A lot of people are sad we're closing," he told a reporter the week before his planned last day in February 1980. "But you put in long hours every day. It gets pretty rough. I'm getting pretty tired."

The day before Mar was to close the restaurant for good, he died of a sudden heart attack at age sixty. His family, many of whom had worked with him at the café, closed it one day early.

KING'S-X (1938)

When White Castle decided to leave Wichita and closed its last hamburger stand, a onetime White Castle manager and fry cook stepped in to continue the legacy on his own terms. A.J. "Jimmie" King, who was trying to pay his way through Wichita Business College, went to work as a line cook at the White Castle on Pattie and Douglas in 1928. He had an entrepreneurial spirit and a strong work ethic, and White Castle owners liked him. They eventually promoted him to plant manager.

A.J. "Jimmie" King took over all the White Castle buildings in 1938 and turned them into King's-X restaurants. Pictured here is the King's-X at First and Broadway. *Jack and Linda Davidson.*

But White Castle decided to leave Wichita and relocate its head office to Columbus, Ohio, and in 1938, the last of the White Castle restaurants closed. King bought the former White Castle hamburger stands at First and Broadway, at Pattie and Douglas and at Hillside and Douglas, changing their names to Kings-X. His business grew quickly, and at one point, King had ten Kings-X hamburger stands in Wichita, most with just room enough for counter seating.

Longtime *Wichita Eagle* food columnist Kathleen Kelly, who died in 2010, fondly remembered eating at those stands as a child. She wrote about them in a 1977 article in the paper: "Standing in line for a seat at the counter of one of the original Kings-X restaurants during World War II is a childhood memory for many Wichitans. The hamburger patties cooked at First and Broadway were thick but the chef piled lots of cooked onions on them and browned the buns on the onion-seasoned grill. Hamburgers were 10 cents each." After visiting a Kings-X hamburger stand, Kelly wrote, the aroma "would attach itself to our hair and coats for several hours."

The inside of an early King's-X diner. *Jack and Linda Davidson.*

In the 1940s, the King family added curb service to its hamburger stands, and during World War II, it added a breakfast menu and started opening twenty-four hours a day to feed factory workers reporting for duty around the clock. Kings-X became known for its flat and crunchy waffles, made from a recipe King had painstakingly developed himself. In the mid-1950s, Kings-X added drive-ins and a drive-through store. Included in its 1950s portfolio was Big Bun, a drive-in restaurant at 4724 East Central that served loose-meat sandwiches on giant hamburger buns. It lasted until the early 1970s. In the 1960s, McDonald's and other competitors arrived in Wichita and started opening restaurants at an alarming rate. The King family wasn't sure how it could compete.

In the early 1970s, the family, now led by A.J.'s son, Wayne, abandoned the hamburger stand business and decided to switch to a full-service restaurant model. In 1973, the family bought Toc's Coffeehouse at George Washington and Harry and switched its remaining two burger stands over to full-service restaurants. Wayne King partnered with local developer George Ablah in 1987

47

to build Jimmie's Diner, a 1950s-era eatery with waitresses in poodle skirts, at 3111 North Rock Road. It served breakfast and lunch, and King described it as a tribute to his father, who died three years later at age ninety-two.

In 2007, Wayne King sold the diner and his last remaining King's-X restaurant, the one at 2014 West Twenty-First Street, to Wichitans Jack and Linda Davidson. They owned the Kings-X building but not the land under it, and in 2012, the landowner sold the lot to CVS Pharmacy. The final King's-X, a throwback building with a zigzag roofline that was built in 1968, met the bulldozers, and Kings-X in Wichita was gone after seventy-four years. Wayne King died of a heart attack in 2007, shortly after he'd sold his restaurants to the Davidsons. In 2011, the Davidsons acquired the Toc's Coffeehouse property. They turned it into a Jimmie's Diner and still run it along with the diner Wayne King founded on Rock Road.

WEST-URN GRILL (1938)

A popular eatery of the 1940s and 1950s was the West-Urn, which operated two restaurants in Wichita. J. Kenneth Parmenter opened the first West-Urn in 1938 at 715 West Douglas. He called it West-Urn Grill, and it operated out of a small prefab structure made by Ablah Hotel Supply Company, whose tiny buildings were precursors to Valentine diners. In its day, the eatery sat one door east of the Civic Theater, a movie palace that operated at 715 West Douglas from 1936 until 1960.

A photo published in the *Wichita Eagle* from inside the West-Urn in 1938 shows a skinny dining room with a low, arched ceiling and a counter lined with stools. The smiling staff is lined up behind the counter, and milkshake machines can be seen behind them. An accompanying story promised free parking, three meals served daily and a special feature of "genuine Italian spaghetti made entirely of choicest imported ingredients including Parmesian [*sic*] cheese, Salonica peppers and imported spaghetti."

That restaurant lasted until 1958. In the meantime, in 1946, another West-Urn opened in a former gas station building at 839 West Thirteenth. The restaurant was called West-Urn Cafe and was sometimes referred to as West-Urn No. 2. A photo from the year it opened shows the façade of the building, still recognizable today, and a big sign in the shape of a metal teapot with a handle that reads "The West Urn." A 1937 Ford is parked in front.

Local lore has it that actress Vera Miles, who lived in Wichita when she was known as Vera Ralston, was a cashier at the restaurant. Miles, who

West-Urn Cafe opened in 1946 in a former gas station building at 839 West Thirteenth. *Wichita– Sedgwick County Historical Museum.*

attended North High School, went on to win the Miss Wichita pageant in 1948 and then became Miss Kansas, earning third place in the Miss America pageant. She went on to star in several films, including Alfred Hitchcock's *The Wrong Man* and *Psycho*. The Thirteenth Street building would go on to house Ed's Cafe, followed by Dick & Jayne's and then Riverside Cafe, which still operates there as of this writing.

DROLL'S ENGLISH GRILL, 1939

In 1932, a Wichita entrepreneur named George Droll partnered with his sister and with onetime Wichita school cafeteria supervisor Annamae

George Droll opened Droll's English Grill at 3120 East Central in 1939. *Wichita–Sedgwick County Historical Museum.*

The interior of Droll's English Grill had an Art Moderne style. *Wichita–Sedgwick County Historical Museum.*

Garvie to open Droll's Restaurant in a space at 117 North Broadway (then called Lawrence), right next door to the Miller Theatre. They operated the restaurant together until 1939, when Droll sold his interest to Garvie and leased a new space at 3120 East Central.

The new Droll's English Grill operated out of a one-story building that had an English pub look from the outside, with Tudor-style dormers and images of horse-drawn carriages hung above the windows. Inside, the new restaurant had an Art Moderne style, and a photo from opening day shows waitresses smiling in neat uniforms, standing next to tables lined with crisp, white tablecloths. The dining room also included a soda fountain and a horseshoe-shaped lunch counter lined with bar stools.

Droll's served "distinctive food," according to early advertisements, and it was open for breakfast, lunch and dinner. Over the years, the successful restaurant was home to many wedding dinners and formal parties. But in 1959, Droll announced that he was retiring from the restaurant business, and he turned the restaurant, by then called Droll's Gourmet, over to two of his longtime employees, sisters Wilma and Verna Bezdek. Droll eventually relocated to Scottsdale, Arizona, and that's where he died in 1972, at age sixty.

RALPH BAUM'S BURGERS (1939)

Ralph Baum opened his first burger stand at 1017 East Douglas around 1939, and he was a purist about his product. The only toppings he would allow were grilled onions, mustard and pickle. That's how a burger was made, as far as he was concerned. Ketchup, remembers his great-niece Janiece Baum Dixon, was not allowed.

He went on to found Ralph Baum's Burger Houses, a series of restaurants opened in Wichita through the 1940s, 1950s and 1960s, including at 2416 East Douglas, 501 North Seneca, 1624 East Thirteenth, 807 East Harry and 3210 East Kellogg. His sixth restaurant was at 424 East Central, where El Patio Cafe is today.

Besides being a burger purist, Baum also hand cut his fries and hand breaded his onion rings. Her uncle's secret, Baum Dixon said, is that he would continually clean his grill and insisted on using only fresh ground beef sold locally by Carl Bell's Meat Market. Customers loved the burgers, which Baum Dixon compares to today's Sport Burger, and they also loved the catchy radio jingles Baum ran on local airwaves.

Ralph Baum was an inventor, too, and family lore has it that he was an early adopter of the carryout concept that invited people to pick up their food at the restaurant but take it home to eat it. He thought about getting a patent on the concept, but he never got around to it.

Ralph Baum came from a food-focused family. His stepmother was an expert baker who would make pies at home and sell them to local restaurants. His brother Banner—who was Baum Dixon's grandfather—owned a restaurant on East Central called Baum Luncheon. Ralph Baum's other brother, Harry, owned a cigar shop in the Eaton Hotel and later one at First and Market. Inside his second cigar shop was a lunch counter, where he sold hot roast beef sandwiches and soup.

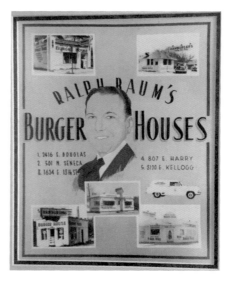

Ralph Baum owned burger stands all over Wichita from the late 1930s to the late 1970s. *Janiece Baum Dixon.*

Ralph Baum held on to his burger restaurants until the mid-1960s, when McDonald's started to take over the burger scene. He then opened a restaurant called Heritage at Hillside and Funston. But he kept that only a couple of years. As his grand finale, he opened a big Ralph Baum's at Harry and Clifton, where a Spangles operates now. After being inducted into the Kansas Restaurant and Hospitality Association's Hall of Fame in 1978, he decided it was time to retire, and he gave up the last Ralph Baum's Burger restaurant the following year. Ralph Baum died in 1986 at age seventy-three.

1940-1949

North Broadway Nightclubs and Barbecue to Go

THE CONNOISSEUR (1942)

A colorized postcard from the 1940s shows an inviting scene: A chef in a toque gazes at the camera, and in front of him, smartly dressed patrons crowd up to the counter to inspect menus while overflowing trays of pastries tempt them just feet away. The restaurant depicted is the Connoisseur, which opened in 1942 at 122 South Market, on the ground floor of the Wheeler-Kelly-Hagny building. The restaurant was owned by Ray Blevins, and its mascot was a mustachioed chef in a kerchief, holding a knife in one hand and a morsel in the other. An article published in the *Wichita Eagle* when the restaurant first opened said it would operate twenty-four hours a day and would specialize in "breakfasts, luncheons and dinners with particular emphasis on sandwiches, salads, steaks" and homemade pastry.

The new restaurant would have a unique "full view kitchen," the article said. All seating would be around an arch-shaped counter, and "everything is cooked right before your eyes. All the facilities are so arranged that every step 'from the ice box to your mouth' is completely visible."

In his 1948 book *I Recommend: Where to Go, Stop, Eat, Play and Shop*, travel writer Roland L. Hill praised the restaurant, calling it one of his favorites. In fact, the type on the back of that colorized postcard brags that the Connoisseur is "Sanctioned by Roland L. Hill" and that "Rolly Knows the Right Places." In the book, Hill notes that Blevins had "reached the conclusion that what the American people want are popular food items, a limited menu, expertly

A postcard shows the interior of The Connoisseur restaurant that operated in the 1940s at 122 South Market, on the ground floor of the Wheeler-Kelly-Hagny building. *Rorabaugh-Millsap.*

prepared and displayed; plus high class dining room atmosphere, served at a well lighted, well decorated, spotless, and comfortable lunch counter."

Hill recollected being stuck in Wichita for a week in 1942 but said that finding The Connoisseur made his stay much more pleasant, and he ate there daily. "Waffles are my favorite food, and here are the finest you will find in many a state. And scrambled eggs." The beautiful restaurant, he concluded, could be the finest in Kansas.

Modern-day Wichitans better remember dining at Blevins's second iteration of The Connoisseur, this one called the Connoisseur Restaurant & Coffee Shop. It opened in 1955 on the lower level of Parklane Shopping Center, Oliver and Lincoln, with seating for 250. A 1957 phone book ad touts the restaurant's charcoal broiled steaks, its homemade breads and pies and its "table d'hote" dinners. It was open for breakfast, brunch, lunch and dinner and known for its family-style fried chicken.

Many Wichtans say they still remember dining at the Parklane restaurant, watching the chefs cook behind the counter and enjoying omelets and pastry carts in the mornings and duck a l'orange in the evenings.

HICKORY HOUSE (1945)

In the 1960s and 1970s, Hickory House at 1635 East Central was where Wichitans went when they were willing to pay a little more for dinner. It served lobster and other upscale dishes and was among Wichita's highest-rated restaurants.

The building where it operated was originally opened just after World War II by Samuel LeDart as LeDart Restaurant, with seating for 55. But in 1950, it was taken over by J. Robert Dry and his wife, Verda, who changed the name to Hickory House. They expanded the restaurant, and it started to earn a national reputation. Not only did the Drys regionally market some of the restaurant's products, like its chicken breading, but they also expanded Hickory House into a business that could serve 310 people at a time. They began offering carryout service in 1961, and in 1964, they added a cafeteria-style snack shop that operated over the lunch hour next door to the restaurant. During that period, Hickory House enjoyed the highest rating of any Wichita restaurant listed in the Mobil Travel Guide, which at the time was quite an honor.

This postcard shows the interior of Hickory House, which was run by J. Robert Dry and his wife, Verda, for nearly two decades. *Rorabaugh-Millsap.*

The Drys ran the restaurant for nearly two decades, selling it in 1967 to Kansas City–based cafeteria operator Myron Green. (The Drys went on to buy and run western wear chain Sheplers, building it into a multimillion-dollar worldwide business.) Hickory House was known for its waitresses wearing long colonial dresses and for cooking its meats over a hickory wood fire. It had a live lobster tank and salad carts that would be wheeled to the individual tables. Also on the menu were items like ham, pork ribs and beef smoked over a hickory pit as well as deep-fried shrimp, Heidelberg kraut, German potato salad and a spinach supreme salad, created by Myron Green and craved by Wichitans for years after the restaurant closed.

In 1970, the Green family, who were Colonial Williamsburg buffs, remodeled the restaurant in that era's motif, adding a wood-burning stone fireplace and oak paneling and decorating five separate dining rooms with colonial antiques. But just before Christmas 1972, a massive fire broke out at the restaurant, resulting in a collapsed roof and $50,000 in damage. The restaurant was rebuilt and opened again in the fall of 1973. The snack shop closed in 1978 to make way for more parking for the main restaurant, and the owners also added a private club that year so that patrons could enjoy a drink while they dined. By 1983, the restaurant had closed.

BROWN'S GRILL (1946)

When they opened it in 1946, Richard and Emma Brown's little restaurant at 545 North Hillside was a twenty-six-seat hamburger stand. Emma famously had to teach her husband, known to his friends as "Brownie," how to fry a hamburger. But over the next four decades, it would grow into a successful family business that included three restaurants being run by the couple and their sons.

Brown's Grill quickly grew from its humble beginnings across the street from Wesley Hospital. By 1949, it had expanded and was selling T-bone steak dinners, which came with a salad, fries, hot rolls and coffee, for ninety-five cents. Fried chicken was another popular menu item. The Browns moved the restaurant to a big new building right next door in 1969, tearing down the original structure to add parking. The new space featured an Old English–style exterior and could seat 425 diners.

In 1966, Brown added a second restaurant—the six-thousand-square-foot Brown's Grill West at 7150 West Harry. It was "chalet-style" and had a wishing well in the back. After the west-side restaurant opened, the flagship became known as Brown's Grill East. It was a place where east-side businesspeople and employees at Wesley could grab a bite, and it also attracted after-game crowds from Wichita State University and nearby high schools. The west restaurant was frequented by airport and aircraft workers and had a Sunday fried chicken special that drew big crowds.

In the summer of 1972, the Brown family added the 504-seat Brown's Cafeteria, which opened on the ground floor of a downtown insurance office at 212 North Market. Brown hired his son Charles to run the restaurant, and on opening day, a city commissioner was on hand to slice the prime rib. The twelve-thousand-square-foot cafeteria made headlines for adopting a

Right: This photo of the sign at Brown's Grill across from Wesley Hospital was taken in 1981. *From the* Wichita Eagle.

Below: Brown's Grill, depicted on this postcard, operated across the street from Wesley Hospital on Hillside. *Rorabaugh-Millsap.*

Brown's Grill West opened at 7150 West Harry in 1965. The caption on the back of this postcard calls the restaurant "The House of Cleanliness." *William J. Schmidt.*

unique-to-Wichita "scrambled pattern" buffet line, which featured a circular setup for the main food line with mini lines all around it. Instead of standing in long lines, people could just walk up to the various stations and ask for what they wanted. Ultimately, the downtown cafeteria wasn't profitable, and it closed almost ten years later.

Brown sold Brown's East and the cafeteria to his sons, Charles, R.J. and Larry, in 1978 and retired in 1984. R.J. Brown was running the east and west restaurants when they closed a day apart in 1987. A note posted that day at Brown's Grill East read: "Because of declining business, the decision to close has been made. It is our feeling that an independent family restaurant cannot operate profitably at this location anymore." In an interview with the *Wichita Eagle-Beacon*, he also pointed to increased competition along the Rock Road corridor.

In 1985, Charles Brown, who had sold his interest in the family restaurants to brother R.J., would go on to open Charley Brown's Restaurant and Lounge at 1443 North Rock Road and later manage other restaurants.

Richard Brown died in 1995, and in his obituary, onetime customers described him as friendly and outgoing but also tough. He would not tolerate white customers in the early 1950s objecting to the admission of Black athletes dining with teammates before and after games.

"Every place else we'd go, we had to stay on the bus and eat, or go into the kitchen and eat," recalled former WSU basketball star Cleo Littleton, who played for the Shockers from 1951 to 1955, in a story about Brown's death that ran in the *Wichita Eagle*. But not at Brown's Grill: "We'd go through the front door. And the food was great...a lot better than a cold hamburger on a bus."

KEN'S KLUB (1946)

Ken's Klub was one of several famous steakhouses and nightspots that opened in the Twenty-Ninth and Broadway area in the 1940s. Its owner was Ken Hill, an Ashland native who became a nationally ranked welterweight boxer during the Depression and went on to serve as an infantry captain in Europe during World War II. His club became one of Wichita's most popular nightspots, reigning through the 1950s and into the 1960s alongside destinations like Savute's, Abe's and Doc's.

Hill was a fixture at his club, and he was known to greet people as they came in and to often allow them back in the kitchen to choose their steaks. He was known for distributing cigars to customers, and his club would often draw visiting celebrities and athletes. He also was known to have built an enormous grill, modeling it after one he'd seen in Germany during the war. It was like a massive George Foreman grill and was said to help seal moisture into his steaks.

Ken's Klub also served garlic salad, and some say Hill may have created the recipe. A menu from the 1960s also lists steak cuts like K.C. club, filet mignon and T-bone. Fried chicken, fried shrimp, filet of sole and stuffed oysters were also served, and Hill was even known to serve deep-fried steak. His homemade bleu cheese salad dressing was famous.

Ken's Klub closed in 1971, and Hill would go on to run Ken's Stockyard Restaurant at the old Wichita Stockyards on Twenty-First Street. The space that held Ken's Klub would in the early 1980s become home to Cortez Mexican Restaurant, which later moved next door and eventually closed. Now, the Ken's Klub space is home to a tortilleria. Ken Hill died in 1998 at age ninety.

ALBERT'S RESTAURANT (1947)

It was known in its later years for black booths, red lacquered walls and a menu that featured not only Cantonese fare but also steaks, prime rib and seafood. And when Albert's Restaurant at 6425 East Kellogg closed in 2001, after fifty-four years in business, it was one of Wichita's last remaining vestiges of the old-school Chinese restaurants that once dotted the city. It was opened in 1947 by Albert Mar, who immigrated to the United States from China as a boy and eventually started a restaurant specializing in his native cuisine. Its first location was on North Hillside, but six years later, he moved it to Kellogg and Woodlawn.

Albert Mar opened Albert's Restaurant in 1954 but sold it to his nephew, Cornell, when he moved to California in 1963. *Cornell Mar.*

At its height, Albert's was considered one of Wichita's nicest restaurants, and it was sometimes patronized by visiting 1940s-era television and film actors like Bob Cummings, star of movies like *The Devil and Miss Jones* and *Dial M for Murder*, and Johnny Weissmuller, who played Tarzan. Albert, however, decided that he wanted to move to California, and in 1963, he sold the restaurant to his nephew, Cornell Mar, who had also immigrated to the United States as a boy.

Cornell, who'd cut his restaurant teeth working in a local steakhouse, ran the 130-seat restaurant until it closed with the help of his wife, Sharon, and children Glenda and Jay. He was known for putting in long hours, and in 1981, he told the *Wichita Eagle-Beacon* that one of the hardest parts of his job was finding cooks who knew how to prepare Cantonese cuisine, which was milder than the fare from northern China. Customers loved dishes like walnut chicken, but Mar would tell the *Wichita Eagle* that he couldn't survive serving only Chinese food, so he also offered a full American menu of steaks and burgers.

Top: Albert's Restaurant operated in Wichita from 1947 until 2001. *Cornell Mar.*

Bottom: Albert's Restaurant closed in 2001 when owners Cornell and Sharon Mar decided to retire. *Cornell Mar.*

The Mars developed a loyal following, even inspiring onetime U.S. representative Dan Glickman to pen a letter to the editor of the *Wichita Eagle* that was published in 1991: "Traveling in China and eating nothing but Chinese food, I realized the Chinese had it all wrong," Glickman wrote. "The best Chinese food in the world was not in China, it was at Albert's Restaurant in Wichita. I was so sure Albert's food was the best, I called him from China to tell him so."

Albert's remained a Wichita favorite over the decades, but eventually, competition in the form of Chinese buffets started moving into Wichita, and the Mars grew tired of their long hours. Their adult children didn't want to take the restaurant over, so the couple quietly decided to close it. Sharon Mar died in 2017, but as of 2021, Cornell Mar still lives in Wichita.

EL CHARRO CAFE (1948)

El Charro Cafe wasn't just a restaurant. It was an experience. Luis Alvarado, who already had Mexican restaurants in Oklahoma City, Dallas, Tulsa and Shreveport, first opened the restaurant in 1948 and told the *Wichita Eagle* that he traveled six thousand miles over seven Mexican states to find authentic fixtures and materials to decorate the interior, which was filled with both tables and booths "upholstered in rust and yellow leather in keeping with the Mexican decoration scheme."

Famously managed by Olegario "Horace" Ayala, the restaurant was known not only for its Mexican food but for the atmosphere as well. Customers went to the restaurant partially to see its fountain, its lighted

El Charro Cafe, which opened in 1948 at 5325 East Kellogg, was managed and co-owned by Olegario "Horace" Ayala. *Wichita–Sedgwick County Historical Museum.*

El Charro Cafe's interior featured a fountain, lighted aquariums built into the walls and a revolving bandstand. *Wichita–Sedgwick County Historical Museum.*

aquariums built into the walls and its organist playing a Hammond B on a revolving bandstand. The flamboyant restaurant sat at 5325 East Kellogg, roughly where Scotch & Sirloin is today.

People say it was Ayala, who also was an owner in the restaurant, who made it what it was. "He was the master at not only arranging the menus and the decor, but he was the greeter par excellence," said Chuck Harris, a longtime friend, in a 1992 obituary published in the *Wichita Eagle.* "Around town, he hobnobbed with all the people who mattered."

The restaurant was a place where people often went for date nights or where they dined before the prom. Celebrities who visited Wichita frequently stopped there, too. Ayala sold the restaurant and moved to Kansas City, where he ran restaurants until he retired in 1985. El Charro Cafe closed in 1972 and was remodeled to become Pat O'Brien's restaurant.

ABE'S CLUB (1948)

It was known for its dark interior and its fluorescent black lighted wall murals of the South Sea Islands. It was also known for its steak, onion rings and garlic salad. Now, Abe's Steakhouse lives only in Wichitans' fond memories. The business closed in 2000, and the building that held it at 1044 West Twenty-Ninth Street North was demolished in 2012.

Abe's roots go back to 1948, when Schafer "Abe" Abraham and his wife, Mabel, bought the forty-seat Longhorn Tavern, which at the time was on Wichita's outskirts but operated near other drinking and dining establishments. For the first two years they owned the tavern, they lived in a shack west of the business. They didn't add food until 1962. But over the years, the couple built Abe's into a 130-seat restaurant frequented by both businessmen and families. Abe's was known for steaks, which Abe hand cut himself while his wife served as hostess. When his sons grew up, they joined the family business as well. Eldest son Don tended bar, and Ron cooked.

An artist named Marvin Norton out of Overland Park painted the well-known glowing scenes of pagodas and palm trees on the restaurant's walls, working on them periodically over a twelve-year period that lasted from the mid-1960s to the late 1970s. The restaurant also had a vintage jukebox that played Frank Sinatra and Glenn Miller tunes and a waitress named Ruby who kept the place afloat.

But illness struck the Abraham family. Abe died in 1977 of lung cancer. His son Ron took over ownership of the club and continued to run it with

Abe's Steakhouse was known for its fluorescent black lighted wall murals of the South Sea Islands. *Sheriann Abraham.*

Mabel Abraham and her son Don are pictured in Abe's Steakhouse in 1985. *From the* Wichita Eagle.

the help of his family—including Mabel—and its height of popularity was in the 1980s. But Don died, also of lung cancer, in 1995 at age forty-seven, as did Ron in 1999 at age forty-eight. The restaurant then was run by Ron's widow, Sheriann. But a year after her husband's death, she decided to close Abe's, much to the disappointment of its decades' worth of regulars. During the last weeks of business in January 2000, people would show up before the doors opened and stand in long lines to get one last taste of Abe's.

A year later, former La Galette owner Tony Abdayem bought the Abe's building and announced plans to open it as Uncle Abe's with a similar menu. The revival, which launched in 2002, was short-lived, though, and Abdayem eventually decided to remove the building. It was torn down in 2012.

BIG BUN (1948)

One of the most popular teen hangouts of the 1950s was Big Bun, a little round drive-in that opened in 1948 at 4724 East Central, on the northwest corner of Central and Oliver. It had a curved lunch counter lined with swiveling chrome stools, and every booth had its own jukebox.

Big Bun was a Kings-X restaurant at 4724 East Central and was a popular stop for teens out cruising in the 1950s. *Jack and Linda Davidson.*

Big Bun served loose meat sandwiches on big hamburger buns plus onion rings, tenderloin sandwiches, chili, fries and waffles that were famous citywide. Its slogan, "Yum Yum Big Bun Try One," was a rhyme no one could forget, and the glowing neon sign was in the shape of a giant hamburger. Kings-X owned Big Bun through its prime, and owners kept it going until 1973, when they lost the lease and put the restaurant up for auction. Today, a QuikTrip operates on the site.

PIT'S BAR-B-Q (1949)

Willie White was not only one of Wichita's best barbecue chefs, but he was also a preacher, a poet and an all-around Wichita character. Known by locals as "Brother Willie," he was often found wearing a red apron and a red-and-white paper cap in his smoke-filled restaurant. White left his job as a butcher at a meatpacking plant in the late 1940s and started a small restaurant at 1704 North Mosley, naming it Pit's Bar-B-Q.

Willie White was the poetry-writing, guitar-picking preacher owner of Pit's Bar-B-Q. *From the* Wichita Eagle.

He built a following and operated there until the early 1970s, when he moved the restaurant to 1003 East First Street. He also opened a restaurant at 2025 South Oliver. White would write out lyrics to his songs and poems on giant sheets of paper and hang them on the walls of his restaurant. In later days, he'd also frequently be found strumming his guitar and singing while his daughter, Mary, took orders. He retired in 1991 and left the restaurant to Mary, who kept Pit's Bar-B-Q going until the late 1990s.

ADAMS BARBECUE (1949)

One of Wichita's most remembered barbecue restaurants was opened in 1949 by Jerome Adams, who had worked for years as a teacher at Dunbar Elementary School. He started his Adams Barbecue on the southwest corner of Seventeenth and Hydraulic as a mostly carryout place and opened it for business Thursdays through Sundays only.

But when it was open, it was a popular lunch stop for local businessmen, who loved the sauce made by Jerome and his wife, Helen. Adams died in 1970, but the restaurant continued until the mid-1980s.

1950-1959

Drive-Ins, Sit-Ins and the Start of Pizza Hut

DOCKUM LUNCH COUNTER (1950)

The lunch counter at the Dockum Drug Store at 111 East Douglas is one of the most famous eateries to operate in Wichita but not because of its menu, which consisted of things like burgers, sandwiches and ice cream sodas. In July 1958, that lunch counter was the site of a historic civil rights sit-in in which two dozen Black students showed up every day from open until close to protest the restaurant's segregation policy and refusal to serve Black patrons at the counter.

They were insulted and tormented, but they persisted, and after three weeks, the drugstore started serving the students, saying it was losing too much money. After that, all Rexall Drug Stores in Kansas were desegregated. The Wichita sit-in was one of the first in the country to succeed, and similar sit-ins happened afterward in places like Oklahoma City. Today, the Ambassador Hotel operates on the site where the Dockum Drug Store once sat.

LANCERS CLUB (1950)

Carpeted walls, Las Vegas–style live shows and dinner and dancing were all hallmarks of the Lancers Club during its heyday in 1970s Wichita. The business got its start in the 1940s, when Vic and Lola Harris, nightclub

The Lancers Club offered food and live music on the basement level of Century Plaza in the 1970s. *From the* Wichita Eagle.

owners known for running popular spots on the outskirts of Wichita like The Stardust and The Rock Castle, took over a building at 138 North Market.

The couple opened a little restaurant called Vic's in the space, but in the early 1950s, after they got their liquor license, they changed the name of the business to the Lancers Club. It was a hit, and in 1965, the Harrises partnered with friend Tom Vickers, who wanted to open a Lancers East at Normandie Shopping Center, Central and Woodlawn. That club lasted into the early 1970s and found success by offering lounge acts that would draw in a healthy nightlife crowd.

In the late 1960s, the Harrises tried to replicate that success by adding a large lounge for live acts in their downtown club. But in February 1971, a blizzard hit Wichita, and fourteen inches of snow accumulated on the downtown Lancers Club lounge's roof. A section of it collapsed, and though no one was injured, the club had to find a new home. That's when the downtown Lancers Club became an iconic symbol of 1970s Wichita.

In 1971, the Harrises spent $250,000 opening Lancers Club in the basement of Century Plaza, 111 West Douglas. Patrons entered through glass double doors just off Finlay Ross Park, the sunken area to the east of Kennedy Plaza that has fountains and where the swimming dragon Christmas character is set up every year.

Inside, the couple built a state-of-the-art Las Vegas–style stage and a bandstand, designed by son and night manager Gregg. Daughter Paula also worked for her parents. Upon the club's opening, the *Wichita Eagle* described the décor as "sophisticated modern" with bright raspberry red carpeting, flocked wallpaper, carpeted and upholstered walls and paint colors ranging from "shocking pink to royal purple." It had a lounge that seated about 270 and a dining room for 140, which was appointed with tables and captains' chairs. There were also two private dining rooms. The club offered nightly entertainment, often drawing well-known comedians, pianists, singers and bands. (Frank Sinatra Jr. played there in 1977.) Patrons would dance the night away.

Lancers Club featured a supper club menu starting at 5:30 p.m. and a lunch buffet from 11:00 a.m. to 2:30 p.m. that had three standard features: prime rib, corned beef and cabbage and baked ham. It was a favorite noontime stop for downtown secretaries, who could catch a lunchtime fashion show every few weeks.

The Lancers Club was not without its difficulties, though. In January 1975, a sixty-three-year-old dishwasher died of a heart attack after she and eight coworkers were held hostage in an early morning robbery. And in the early 1970s, the club was among several accused of racial discrimination in approving members. (The club had about one thousand members in 1976.) The Harrises denied those allegations.

The Lancers Club was closed by May 1984, and another club called Spritzers moved in. For some time afterward, a Lancers East operated at 7335 East Kellogg in the penthouse of the Holiday Inn, and the founders' son, Gregg—who was also a musician—would perform there. It lasted only a couple of years, but the memory of the Lancers Club lives on with fans across Wichita, who still reminisce about going there for special occasions with their parents—and about occasionally ending up in the fountain outside at the end of a particularly rowdy night.

SIDMAN'S (1951)

He started his restaurant career working as a soda jerk in Alva, Oklahoma. But in 1939, Jack Sidman landed a job at the famous Dockum Drug Store in Wichita, and he spent eleven years there, eventually being promoted to oversee the chain's fountain and luncheonette departments.

By 1951, Sidman was his own boss, and over the next three decades, he built a small Wichita-based dining empire that at one time would include nineteen different eateries across the state. His first restaurant was Sidman's Downtowner at 128 North Market, which Jack opened in 1951, specializing in broasted chicken. Four years later, he bought another restaurant, this one called South Seas at 1601 East Douglas, and that's where he first offered the new "serva-teria" concept. A waitress would deliver silverware, beverages, hot rolls and desserts to the tables, and then diners would help themselves to a bar featuring more than fifteen salads, hot foods and vegetables.

It was a popular concept, and Sidman would go on to open restaurants in Kansas towns like Coffeyville, Hesston, Newton and Independence and even one in Colorado. Among the many Wichita restaurants he owned were Sidman's Boulevard at 908 George Washington Boulevard, Sidman's Sunset at 940 South West Street and Sidman's Uptowner at 3201 East Douglas. In 1973, as Sidman's restaurant chain was celebrating its twenty-second anniversary, he estimated that he'd served nine million people and cooked more than three million pounds of chicken.

A postcard shows Sidman's on South Seneca, which was the last of Wichita's several restaurants founded by Jack Sidman to close. *Don Eastman Photography.*

Among his longest-lasting eateries was Sidman's Western restaurant, which opened at 6601 West Kellogg in 1955 and featured waitresses sporting short skirts and cap pistols. The restaurant's buffet became a big draw, especially at the holidays, and famous band man Lawrence Welk used to dine there when he visited Wichita. The restaurant, with its dark wood paneling and red tablecloths, closed in 1983.

Jack Sidman was known as a kind man and a good cook who was particular about presentation in his restaurants. His wife, Ruby, was a five-foot-tall spitfire who was famous for chasing down those who dared try to rob her restaurants. Once, she held on to a fleeing robber's car door handle as he tried to get away. Another time, she pinned a purse snatcher against a wall with her car. By 1983, the Sidmans were in debt, victims of the economy, aircraft layoffs and increased competition from fast-food restaurants, they said. They closed their last restaurant at 2532 South Seneca in July of that year.

DOC'S STEAKHOUSE (1952)

Doc's Steakhouse has been gone since 2014, but people are still dreaming about, talking about and searching out the recipe for its famous garlic salad—and they probably always will be.

Dwight L. Hustead, the son of a Nebraska doctor, opened the restaurant in 1952 inside a building at 1515 North Broadway that had just a small cooking and dining area. His nickname was "Doc." At the time, North Broadway was the main entertainment district in Wichita, and Doc's was one of many popular supper clubs of the time. Ken's Klub, Abe's and Savute's, which still remains, were its contemporaries.

Doc is another Wichita restaurateur who sometimes gets credit for originating the famous garlic salad, which in 1977, *Wichita Eagle* food writer Kathleen Kelly described as "the most distinctive salad in Wichita. It's a blend of chopped vegetables in a creamy dressing redolent with garlic served atop a modicum of shredded lettuce."

The menu also included items like pan-fried chicken livers and gizzards; one-inch-thick prime rib, which the cook would only prepare rare; chicken fried steak; frog legs; shrimp; french fried clam strips; catfish; pork chops; fried shrimp; spaghetti and meatballs; and lasagna.

The restaurant changed hands in 1963, when Mike Belluomo and Louis Scott bought it from Scott's neighbor, Hustead. Over the years, they kept

Doc's Steakhouse at 1515 North Broadway was abandoned in 2014 and still sits empty. *Travis Heying.*

adding on to the building, culminating in a 1970 renovation that tied the many parts together into a cozy and rustic space. The redo included the addition of dark-stained oak paneling on the walls as well as new carpet, booths, tables and chairs. That's also when the building's façade of stone, cedar siding and shake shingles was added, along with the entry arch for the parking lot that can still be seen today on the abandoned building.

The restaurant remained a Wichita favorite for decades, and in 2014, it was being run by Brian Scott, the grandnephew of former owner Louis Scott. Brian had grown up working in the restaurant and said he dreamed of modernizing and reviving it. But he was never able to make enough money, and he closed the restaurant in October 2014.

One interesting tidbit from Doc's history: in 1974, the owners filed suit against television station KAKE-TV for a story it had produced the year before in which it followed a state health inspector who was inspecting the kitchen. During the visit, the inspector found thirty-seven violations. The owners maintained that the station misled them, saying they were producing a documentary in which they were following a health inspector as he did his work. The report set the restaurant up for public ridicule, the owners said, and customers stopped coming, resulting in a loss of nearly $50,000. The case went to trial in 1977, and the restaurant eventually lost. The Kansas Court of Appeals upheld the jury verdict in 1979.

THE CEDAR (1952)

Perhaps no ham sandwich has ever been more famous than the ham sandwich made by The Cedar. At least not in Wichita. Brothers Tom and Ted Werts opened the bar and restaurant in 1952 in a building at 3906 East Thirteenth Street, just six blocks south of Wichita State University. It became a popular hangout for college students, especially Greeks and football players. The inside looked like a typical bar and was furnished with cedar tables that the owners imported from Missouri. Regulars were fond of carving their names into a big round cedar table that was a fixture in the restaurant for decades. Graduates would return year after year to make sure they could still find their signatures.

In the early days, the menu was small and featured ham, liverwurst and cheese sandwiches on rye or white bread. The sandwich that became the most popular, though, was the ham sandwich that was piled high on rye and dressed with mustard.

Larry Adair (*left*) bought The Cedar in the early 1980s. Here he's seen sitting at its famous cedar table into which regulars would carve their names. *From the* Wichita Eagle.

The Cedar's identity changed over the years, and by the 1970s, it had become Wichita's first punk rock mecca. Bands like the Embarrassment would draw huge crowds on Saturday nights, sometimes nearly four times the size of the restaurant's sixty-eight-person capacity. Barroom brawls were not an unusual occurrence. In 1982, restaurateur Larry Adair bought The Cedar, and punk rock was banned. He turned it into a quieter lunch destination, carpeting the tile floors and filling the room with plants and brass ceiling fans. It became a favorite dining destination of WSU faculty and nearby Wesley Medical Center staffers on lunch breaks. WSU students would still hang out in the evenings.

Although the punk rock patrons of the 1970s bemoaned the change, Adair did drag out of storage that round cedar table that had once been so popular with patrons but had been hidden away by a previous owner. He situated it on the stage, which was no longer being used. By the early 2000s, The Cedar was more of a neighborhood bar and a destination for Shocker loyalists, who would often gather for a drink and a sandwich before going to basketball games at nearby Koch Arena. Brothers David and Terry Baker took over The Cedar in 2003, and three years later, they decided to move it. They abandoned the legendary bar's longtime home on Thirteenth and took over the space in Brittany Center, Twenty-First and Woodlawn, that Tanner's Bar & Grill had just vacated. They wanted to expand, they said, and to serve more than just sandwiches. The kitchen at the original building wouldn't allow for that. In 2007, the Bakers completed the move, but regulars said they missed the original spot. The Bakers hauled over booths and tables from the old space, including the famous carved table, but the magic was gone. One year later, The Cedar was closed.

KAU KAU KORNER (1952)

Chuck Schoenhofer and Hugh Stevens were friends and brothers-in-law, and both were traveling salesmen in the 1950s. They knew nothing about the restaurant business. But in November 1952, they teamed up to purchase Kau Kau Korner, a small restaurant that had already been operating for a few years at 3002 East Central, near the corner of Hillside and Central.

At first, the restaurant sold things like chicken fried steaks, open-face beef sandwiches, pork tenders, shrimp dinners, onion rings and milkshakes. Its specialty was a burger called the Chobby Champ, basically a Big Mac before the Big Mac existed. People could get their food delivered to their cars by a

Left: Chuck Schoenhofer (*right*) is pictured here with his wife, Peg, during the early days of his restaurant, Kau Kau Korner, at 3002 East Central. *Mary Ann Schoenhofer.*

Below: Chuck Schoenhofer (*right*) and Hugh Stevens (*far left*) were Wichita's first Kentucky Fried Chicken franchisees. They're pictured here with KFC founder Harland Sanders and Clark Stevens (*second from right*). *Mary Ann Schoenhofer.*

carhop or eat inside, and the restaurant would often tout its air conditioning in its advertisements. The 1950s were the heyday years for Kau Kau Korner, Schoenhofer's family remembers today. It drew customers from all walks of life, including doctors, lawyers, athletes and families. The actor who played Doc Stone in *Gunsmoke* visited more than once, and his autographed picture hung on the wall.

Eventually, owners Schoenhofer and Stevens visited a Kentucky Fried Chicken restaurant in Lawrence and were amazed by what they tasted. In 1960, they became Sedgwick County's first Kentucky Fried Chicken franchisees. They added the chicken to their menu right away and changed the name of the restaurant to Kau Kau Kentucky Fried Chicken. Back then, franchisees were given KFC founder Harland Sanders's secret recipe with eleven herbs and spices as well as a pot just the right size to cook two chickens in shortening. Sanders would travel around and visit each of the restaurants to check on their quality. The Schoenhofer family still has a photo of Chuck Schoenhofer and Hugh Stevens posing with the legendary chicken man.

Fried chicken soon became the restaurant's top seller, and Schoenhofer and Stevens opened another Kau Kau Chicken at 1225 West Douglas, then another at 2501 East Harry. In the mid-1960s, they changed their restaurants over to full Kentucky Fried Chicken franchises, selling jumbo boxes of chicken for $2.25. The duo also owned a couple of Kau Kau Roast Beef restaurants in the early 1970s: one at South Hydraulic and Pawnee and one at 6125 East Kellogg.

When Stevens's adult sons began working for the company in the 1970s, they decided to split their business interests. In 1977, Schoenhofer turned the original Kau Kau Korner into Kau Kau Burger. The concept didn't last, though, and he eventually sold the building.

During his life, Schoenhofer would own many KFC restaurants and continued to do so until he retired and left the business to his son, Denis, who is still a KFC franchisee. Chuck died in 2006 at age eighty-five, just a month after he celebrated his forty-sixth year as a KFC franchisee.

Stevens died in 1994 at age eighty-two. His son, Jim, became a successful restaurateur, too. He owned Big Cheese Pizza restaurants and was an early franchisee of Applebee's. He just sold his twenty-two Applebee's restaurants, including the ones in Wichita, in 2020. He still owns a few Freddy's Frozen Custard & Steakburgers franchises.

MAR'S GARDEN (1953)

A full-page ad in the May 28, 1953 edition of the *Wichita Beacon* shows a photo of Young Mar dressed in a suit and tie and smiling warmly. The ad also includes a photo of the new Mar's Garden Restaurant, set to celebrate its grand opening the next day. Mar, who opened the restaurant at 2407 East Harry with partner Wah Mar, was a Chinese immigrant with a familiar story. In 1920, when he was just seven, he immigrated with his mother to San Francisco, where his family owned an import/export business specializing in salted fish, spices and produce.

When he was nineteen, he traveled back to his village and married Shan Yung "Susie" Wong in an arranged marriage. But because of the Chinese Exclusion Act, he could not take her back to the United States. He spent the next twenty-four years trying to get her and his children, who were conceived during his visits back home, cleared to join him. He was not successful until 1957.

In the meantime, he became a restaurant cook and settled in Kansas, where in 1952, he and Wah Mar opened a restaurant called The Circle in Junction City. A favorite with soldiers at nearby Fort Riley, The Circle was a success and enabled the partners to expand into Wichita.

Young Mar (*center*) was the owner of Mar's Gardens Restaurant at 2407 East Harry. He's pictured here in the restaurant with his daughters Linda (*left*) and Goldie (*right*). *Linda Tse.*

In 1953, they opened Mar's Bar-B-Que in the building on East Harry. They expanded the restaurant and changed its name to Mar's Garden in 1953. Young Mar's wife and two daughters, Linda and Goldie, finally joined him in Wichita four years later. His baby, Edward, did not join the family until 1964, when he was eight years old.

Young Mar oversaw the daily operations at Mar's Garden and loved to bring his two daughters to work. The restaurant served, like all early Chinese restaurants, a menu that featured Americanized Chinese dishes like chicken chow mein and sweet-and-sour pork rolls as well as American favorites like fried chicken and burgers. Mar's Garden was filled with comfortable booths and a counter lined with stools, and the walls featured dragons and bamboo stalks hand-painted by Young Mar himself.

He was a consummate host, remembered his eldest daughter, Linda Tse, and customer service was his strong suit. He always carried a Chinese-to-English dictionary in his pocket, in case he needed it. "He was the one that wrote the book on customer service, maybe to the extreme," she said. "He was very generous with his customers, and some took advantage of him."

Young Mar and Wah Mar sold Mar's Garden to their chefs in 1972 and soon also sold The Circle. Young Mar died suddenly of a heart attack in 1975. He was just sixty-two years old. Different owners kept Mar's Garden going until 1990.

FORUM CAFETERIA (1954)

People who grew up in Wichita during the 1950s and 1960s fondly remember the Forum Cafeteria, which opened at 115 South Market in October 1954. It was an especially popular place for families to dine after church on Sundays, and many remember stopping there for a meal after shopping at downtown department stores like Innes Department Store and Macy's. For some, lunch at the Forum was part of a Christmas shopping tradition. The Forum Cafeteria chain started in Kansas City, Missouri, where in 1921, the first Forum opened at 1220 Grand Avenue. At the chain's height, there were fourteen locations across the country, including in Denver, Chicago and Los Angeles. Its founder, Clarence Hayman, died in 1971.

During its heyday in Wichita, the Forum Cafeteria was the highest-volume restaurant in town, serving more than 3,500 customers each day. Many nearby businesspeople were known to eat at the cafeteria every day

The Forum Cafeteria opened at 115 South Market in 1954. *Wichita–Sedgwick County Historical Museum.*

of the week. People were drawn to the Forum Cafeteria, which operated on two stories, because of its specialty of "home cooked meals for reasonable prices." Wichitans still wax nostalgic about the cafeteria's chicken pot pies, gelatin salads, fried potatoes and boysenberry pie. Many remember working their first jobs at the cafeteria, and they still swap stories online about the dumbwaiter that would transport dishes from the top level to the bottom to be washed. Forum Cafeteria operated near the Dockum Drug Store at Douglas and Broadway, where in 1958, local students staged a historic lunch counter sit-in protesting segregation. Local historians say that at the time, the Forum was one of the few places in Wichita that would serve African American patrons.

A retrospective published in the *Wichita Eagle* in 1978 said that, for the Forum's grand opening, orchids were flown in from Hawaii and given to every female customer. Hundreds of people lined up to be among the first customers served. But over the years, downtown became less of a shopping destination, and business at the Forum dried up. It served its last meal on May 31, 1973.

ELIZABETH'S RESTAURANT (1955)

Elizabeth Huey, who founded Elizabeth's Restaurant at 504 South Bluff in 1955, was one of Wichita's earliest solo female restaurant owners. Born in Atchison, Kansas, Huey earned a degree from Kansas State University in dietetics and institutional management in 1939. After several internships and restaurant jobs in other cities, she returned to Wichita in 1953 and was briefly a partner in Wolf's Cafeteria. But two years later, she opened her own place in a former service garage at Kellogg and Bluff.

The restaurant, which at different times was also referred to as Elizabeth's Fine Foods and Elizabeth's Tea Room, served tearoom-style fare. Many Wichitans still remember dressing up and wearing gloves to go there and indulging in desserts like ice cream pie, chocolate meringue pie and baked Alaska. Some remember ordering the restaurant's "surprise entree," agreeing to eat whatever the staff delivered to the table. Chicken à la King and fruit salad with "special dressing" were among some of the favorites.

The interior was novel for its day and featured an indoor garden with a picket fence, sweet potato vines and lots of potted plants. There were brick walls, concrete floors and tables covered in white tablecloths. An old postcard from the restaurant that's still circulating shows a dining room

Elizabeth's Restaurant, shown in this old postcard, operated at the corner of Kellogg and Bluff and was owned by Elizabeth Huey. *Dick Azim Studios.*

filled with midcentury light fixtures, and the caption on the back describes Elizabeth's as having a "sea-coast atmosphere." An article printed in the *Wichita Eagle* around 1960 (and then dutifully reprinted in full in the *Atchison Daily Globe*) describes Elizabeth's as "a meeting place for Wichitans of nearly every strata."

It quoted Huey as saying she preferred to use women cooks because "they care a little bit more." The restaurant, the article said, had "a simple and unpretentious atmosphere, waitresses who are attentive and cuisine which is better tasted than described." Huey was also an attentive owner, and she even earned the Kansas Restaurant & Hospitality Association's Restaurateur of the Year award in 1963. She was known for decorating Elizabeth's at Christmas and would have her brother, Ben—a professor of forest economics in Colorado—ship her giant trees that would stretch to the ceiling.

In 1964, Huey married Reid McLain of Indianapolis and announced plans to move with him. Though she helped him run his successful ice cream mold business called Snow Bird, she flew back and forth from Wichita so she could continue managing Elizabeth's. That continued until 1968, and the restaurant closed for good on Christmas Eve 1972. The following year, another soon-to-be iconic Wichita restaurant—Portobello Road—moved into the space.

AUNTIE SWEET'S BAR-B-QUE (1956)

Auntie Sweet was Mathilda Dunbar, a Mississippi native who moved to Wichita and opened a barbecue restaurant at 1019 East Murdock. Her specialties were soul food, fried chicken and chitterlings as well as beef brisket, hotlinks, ham and ribs. People remember Dunbar as a fan of blues

music, and she would often play her favorite—B.B. King—on the jukebox in the dining room. The restaurant lasted through the mid-1990s.

Mathilda Dunbar was the popular owner of Auntie Sweet's Bar-B-Que, which opened in 1956 at 1019 East Murdock. *From the* Wichita Eagle.

PIZZA HUT (1958)

One of Wichita's biggest culinary claims to fame is that it is the birthplace of Pizza Hut. In 1958, brothers Dan and Frank Carney were students at what is now Wichita State University, and they converted a former beer tavern at Kellogg and Bluff into a five-hundred-square-foot pizza restaurant.

The brothers had to borrow $600 from their mother to start the place, and they chose the name Pizza Hut because only eight letters would fit on their sign. At the time, Frank Carney was nineteen, and Dan was twenty-six and working on his MBA. In their first days of business, they used a cigar box for a cash register.

The restaurant took off, and by 1959, the brothers had three Wichita locations. They started franchising that year, and within a decade, there were more than three hundred Pizza Huts operating across the globe under the restaurant's signature red roof. By 1971, Pizza Hut was the number-one pizza restaurant chain in the world, both in total restaurants and sales.

The first Pizza Hut opened in 1958 in a five-hundred-square-foot former beer tavern in Wichita. *Pizza Hut.*

Then, in 1977, the brothers sold Pizza Hut to PepsiCo. for $300 million, and the chain continued to grow.

Frank Carney, who died in December 2020 at age eighty-two, went on to become a Papa John's franchisee in the 1990s and was one of the company's biggest franchisees. In 1997, he starred in a national commercial for Papa John's in which he famously uttered the sentence, "Sorry guys: I found a better pizza." He took on other ventures, too, including restaurants like Western Sizzlin, real estate and oil and gas. As of this writing, Dan Carney still lives in Wichita as he approaches his nineties.

Though PepsiCo. moved the Pizza Hut headquarters to Dallas in 1995, Wichita still has a strong attachment to the company. In addition to several major Pizza Hut franchisees still existing in the area, the original Pizza Hut building was moved to a new spot on the WSU campus in 2017 and turned into a Pizza Hut museum. Among the items on display at the museum, which opened in April 2018, are a napkin featuring the recipe for the original Pizza Hut sauce written in Dan Carney's hand as well as the original restaurant's first work schedule.

PART II

THE MODERN DINING SCENE EMERGES

1960-1969

Steaks, Fondue and Beef on Buns

FIFE AND DRUM (1960)

The building had a roof some Wichitans have aptly described as "squiggly," and that's just one of the reasons many still remember Fife and Drum, a family restaurant that Pat and Steve Xidis operated out of the Wishbone Building at 5231 East Central. Erected in 1924, the building first held a bootleg roadhouse, and legend has it that a lookout would be stationed in the little window at the top of the wishbone-shaped roof, watching out for police. After, the building was home to other restaurants, including one of Wichita's early Italian eateries called Roma Cafe. But the Xidis family took it over in 1960 and opened Fife and Drum, a homey restaurant that was known for its fried chicken, short ribs, sandwiches, cinnamon rolls and lemon meringue pie.

People who dined there as children fondly remember that Fife and Drum had a candy counter at the front, and the owners and waitresses would often give little ones treats if they were well behaved. Long licorice ropes were a favorite.

Wichita loved owner Steve Xidis, the son of Greek immigrants, who moved to Wichita from California in

Steve Xidis was the affable owner of Fife and Drum, which operated in Wichita's historic Wishbone Building. *From the* Wichita Eagle.

1923. He partnered with his brother, George, to run a few other restaurants before Fife and Drum, including Poulos Grill at 110 East Douglas and G&S Lunch at 114 East First. After serving in the army infantry during World War II, he opened Steve's Candy Shop at 1411 East Douglas and ran it for fifteen years.

He opened Fife and Drum with his wife, Pat, and the two were well known for their much-loved restaurant. As they aged, they wanted to retire, twice trying to close the business only to bend to customer pleas and reopen. In 1981, they reopened Fife and Drum at 9100 East Kellogg. Then they moved to 600 North Andover Road in Andover and finally closed the restaurant in 1989.

Today, the famous Wishbone Building that held Fife and Drum—also home to La Palma in the 1980s and Jet Bar-B-Q in the 1990s—is just a memory. It was dismantled at the behest of Wichita's Historical Preservation Alliance in 1998, when property owner and Pizza Hut founder Frank Carney wanted it removed to make way for a new strip center. It was stored in pieces in a lot in Old Town but sat there too long and became an eyesore. In 1999, the city said it had to be moved. At one time, the alliance had big plans for reassembling and using the historic building, suggesting they might turn it into a tourist information center. But the deteriorating pieces now sit in an outdoor storage facility on Wichita's south side.

SANDY'S DRIVE-IN (1960)

Another drive-in popular with Wichita teens in the 1960s was Sandy's Drive-In, a national chain that was founded in Illinois in 1956 and was an early McDonald's competitor. But the owners eventually sold out to Hardee's, and by 1973, most of the Sandy's restaurants across the country had been converted. In May 1973, ceremonies in Wichita marked the switch over of Wichita's nine remaining Sandy's to Hardee's restaurants.

Sandy's mascot was a smiling young woman wearing a plaid beret, and among its famous burgers was the "Big Scot," a "giant of a meal" that was similar to a Big Mac. Its toppings included chopped cabbage and a special sauce. Many diners also remember ordering HiLo burgers, which featured two patties with cheese in the middle.

Over the years, Sandy's operated in Wichita at addresses including 3006 South Seneca, 1909 East Pawnee, 9111 West Central, 1140 South Seneca, 201 East Douglas, 4601 East Thirteenth and 5207 East Kellogg. A Sandy's that operated at Douglas and Grove often served as the east-side turnaround spot for teens "dragging Douglas." North High School students would hang out at the Sandy's at 456 West Thirteenth Street. The former Sandy's building at 3006 South Seneca, with its recognizable zigzag roofline, stood until 2013, holding a Bosley's Tires store, among other businesses. It was torn down to make way for a medical center.

GRIFF'S BURGER BAR (1960)

Griff's Burger Bar is another hamburger chain that, like White Castle, was founded in Wichita but eventually disappeared from the city. H.J. Griffith opened the first restaurant in March 1960 and served hamburgers, cheeseburgers, sodas, fries and shakes. By 1965, there were sixty-five Griff's locations, and at one time, they were all across the nation. Many Griff's operated just off of highway exits. The earliest Griff's Burger Bar restaurants operated out of portable A-frame Valentine diner structures produced in Wichita and had drive-through windows and big signs featuring Griffy, the company's clown-like mascot with a chef's hat and stars for eyes.

Over the years, Griff's operated at several Wichita addresses, including 2357 South Hydraulic, 1550 South Oliver, 2908 East Kellogg, 214 West Twenty-First Street South, 2460 South Seneca and 540 North West. The Griff's chain is still around today and has twelve remaining restaurants in New Mexico, Louisiana and Texas.

CHATEAU BRIAND (1961)

It was one of Wichita's most high-end restaurants, and only people who could afford to order steak and other luxury entrées without knowing the prices dined there with frequency. But Chateau Briand was a Wichita favorite that survived more than thirty years, various owners and even a relocation. It opened in 1961 in a converted white farmhouse with a green roof at 10603 East Kellogg. The owner was Everett Jabara, a prolific Wichita restaurateur who over the years also had places like The Famous, Angel's and Rock Road Cafe. Chateau Briand didn't offer a printed menu. Instead, staff members would roll a cart to the table with samples of various menu items, and diners would choose what they wanted—without knowing what it would cost—and many of those dishes would be dramatically set aflame. One of the most popular selections was the restaurant's namesake dish, chateaubriand, which featured medallions of beef served with a flaming mushroom and wine sauce. T-bone, ribeye and strip steaks also were available, as were kabobs and seafood dishes.

The restaurant could seat two hundred and was divided into several dining rooms that were decorated in shades of brown, gold and beige with wood paneling on the walls and heavy drapes on the windows. The lights were kept dim with a glow provided by chimney lamps at the tables.

Restaurateur Anthony Miller took over the restaurant in 1977, and after that, it was frequently called Anthony Miller's Chateau Briand. In 1993, Miller relocated the restaurant to the Tudor Inn at 9100 East Kellogg. But he told people he didn't like the new location, and it didn't last long. The restaurant was closed for good by 1996.

SHAKEY'S PIZZA PARLOR (1963)

They were part of a national chain, but in the 1960s and 1970s, Wichita's two Shakey's Pizza Parlors were also part of the fabric of the city. Shakey's was founded in Sacramento, California, in 1954, and in the 1960s, it started to expand across the country. Wichita's restaurants were part of R.V. "Vince" Wells's Wells Pizza Inc., which had a dozen franchises all over Kansas and in Des Moines and Omaha, too. Shakey's, considered to be the country's first pizza chain, peaked in the mid-1970s, when it had five hundred restaurants across the United States.

Wells told the *Wichita Beacon* in 1969 that when he decided to franchise Shakey's, he'd eaten exactly two pizzas in his life and hadn't liked either one. "They either had too thick and doughy a crust or they were too spicy for my taste," he said. "But then I ate my first Shakey's pizza and I fell in love with it." Wells opened the first Wichita Shakey's in June 1963 at 1343 North Oliver, followed a year later by another one at 1140 West Pawnee. In 1974, a fancy new Shakey's opened at 430 North Rock Road, replacing the restaurant on North Oliver.

Shakey's, whose signs featured a portly chef and the words "Shakey's Pizza Parlor & Ye Public House," was a popular family hangout that offered thin-crust pizzas made in 750-degree ovens with toppings like eastern Polish sausage, imported anchovies, shrimp and oysters as well as more common toppings like pepperoni, sausage and mushrooms. The restaurants typically had two dining rooms—one for families and one just for grownups—and the grownups enjoyed drinking dark beer when they visited. Shakey's was known for live entertainment and often featured musical acts playing ragtime on piano and banjo. Many Wichitans remember that the Thirteenth and Oliver Shakey's had a player piano inside. The restaurant would also project black-and-white movies for its customers, and in Wichita, Shakey's was a popular Friday night hangout for local teens. Kids would often have their birthday parties at Shakey's and walk away with one of its signature Styrofoam straw hats. The employees wore those hats, too, as well as striped shirts and string ties. The Shakey's Pizza chain still exists and has locations in California and Washington State.

LAZY-R (1963)

In 1963, Wichita entrepreneur George Stevens Jr. and his partner, Harvey Rosen, opened their first Lazy-R, a western-themed restaurant at 5405 East Central, where they sold quarter-pound burgers and charcoal hamburger steaks. The restaurant's mascot, Sheriff Regrub (burger spelled backward), was a favorite of young visitors, and many Wichitans still remember eating at Lazy-R with their families as kids.

Over the years, the chain grew. By the time the last Lazy-R closed in 1989, Stevens and Rosen had operated six locations, including at 2544 South Seneca and 608 North Broadway in Wichita. They also had Lazy-Rs in Topeka and Manhattan. It was November 1969 when they opened their Lazy-R Charco at 7805 West Kellogg, and it was their fourth and biggest Wichita restaurant. It could seat 125 in the dining room and had a private party room that could accommodate just as many. It featured lots of western-themed touches, including light fixtures crafted from wagon wheels and replicas of branding irons. Full-sized chuck wagons were used for décor both inside and outside. And customers who visited were greeted by a unique roofline that featured three pointed peaks.

After ordering at the counter, diners would take a seat in one of the restaurant's wooden colonial-style chairs and wait for a number to be called. People loved the burgers, and particularly popular were the chili cheeseburgers and the No. 4, The Bronco, topped with hickory sauce, pickles and cheese. Onion rings, hamburger steaks, apple dumplings and banana fritters were also in demand. Kids loved The Yearling, a tiny burger with a sucker stuck into it.

Though Lazy-R was popular for more than twenty-five years, Stevens closed the last remaining restaurant, the original on East Central, in 1989. After that, he assisted his daughters in their various restaurant projects. In 1989, after he closed on East Central, Stevens added some of Lazy-R's most popular menu items to his daughters Brandi's and Tara's Pappy's Restaurant at 545 North Hillside. The following year, the family changed the restaurant's name to Pappy's Lazy-R. In 1994, Brandi and Tara opened a Lazy-R revival at 7088 East Kellogg. It was a full-service restaurant with a bar, a soda fountain and an all-day breakfast menu. By 1998, that space was home to Wichita's first Red Bean's Bayou Grill. In the early 2000s, Stevens also helped Brandi run the Old Oxford Mill Restaurant in Oxford, Kansas. George Stevens Jr. died in 2007 at age seventy-five. Rosen died in 2014 at age eighty-three.

RUDY'S BBQ (1965)

By the time Rudy Nicholson died in 2005, he was known not only as one of Wichita's best barbecue chefs but also as a savvy businessman who also ran a car dealership: Nicholson Motors at Thirteenth and Hydraulic. But he's best remembered for Rudy's BBQ, which he opened at 2404 East Ninth Street in 1965.

The restaurant was in an old filling station, and friends loaned Nicholson $2,000 to buy the space. (After he closed the restaurant, Nicholson said he paid the loan back in $50-a-month installments.) For thirty-six years, his restaurant was a Wichita favorite known for its takeout barbecue beef, ribs and more. Rudy's was a favorite among other local car dealers, who would get big catering orders to reward their salesmen.

He ran the restaurant with his wife, Ruth, until 2001. He died of lung cancer in 2005.

LAKESHORE CLUB (1965)

In October 1965, a full-page advertisement ran in the *Wichita Beacon* announcing the grand opening of the Lakeshore Club, a new private club and restaurant that bordered a sandpit lake at 3800 South Seneca. At the time, though, the owners referred to the small body of water bordered by I-235 as "Crystal Lake." Opening-day festivities were to include skydivers who would land in the lake, a water ski show, live Hawaiian music and a luau with a "genuine Hawaiian roast pig" prepared on the beach. Photos in the ad depicted the exterior of the clubhouse and also the inside of the Tiki Room, a beach-level room for music and dancing furnished in Hawaiian décor. There was also a photo of the main club lounge, which included a bar and swiveling bucket chairs.

Many Wichitans say they remember that their families were members of the club and that the kids could swim all day while mom and dad enjoyed gin and tonics and hamburgers on the beach—an unusual luxury in landlocked Kansas. Some remember eating in the upscale restaurant on special occasions or during company Christmas parties. The Lakeshore Club had an occasional seafood buffet, and it was the first place many Wichitans ever sampled frog legs.

A menu from the 1980s lists higher-end dishes like flaming chateaubriand for two, steak and lobster tail, breaded oysters and Alaskan king crab legs. The cocktail menu included Brandy Alexanders, White Russians and the like.

Sampson Enterprises put the club up for auction in late 1985, and in 1986, Vern Miller—a former Kansas attorney general, Sedgwick County sheriff and district attorney—bought it. He owned it for only a year before selling it. By 1988, a restaurant called On the Waterfront had taken over the space, and the Lakeshore Club was no more. The space held a series of restaurants over the years, including Brews Brothers Grill and Icehouse in the late 1990s. Then, in 2018, city officials announced plans to raze the old building. There's now an inflatable water park called Splash Aqua Park in "Crystal Lake."

GEORGIE PORGIE PANCAKE SHOP (1966)

In the 1960s, movie theater owner and Lebanese immigrant George Laham decided to open a restaurant. He named it after himself, calling it Georgie Porgie Pancake Shop. The restaurant operated in the corner of Normandie Center at Central and Woodlawn in the same spot where Cafe Asia operated through the end of 2020. In addition to pancakes, it sold shish kebabs and fried chicken, and it developed a loyal following.

In 1971, Laham sold Georgie Porgie to Wayne Wong, a World War II veteran who had moved to Wichita in 1935 at age thirteen and had grown up working for his father, Tung Jing Mar, at Pan-American Cafe, the popular chop suey restaurant that opened in downtown Wichita in 1917. Wong,

Georgie Porgie Pancake Shop was owned by Wayne Wong (*left*), whose father, Tung Jing Mar, was an early owner of Pan-American Cafe. Wong is pictured here with his son, Edward. *Edward Wong.*

though, had become a restaurateur in his own right, having run the T-Bone Supper Club at Forty-Seventh and South Broadway, and he was looking for a business that he and his wife, Kim Suey Wong, could run together.

During the 1970s and 1980s, Georgie Porgie was one of Wichita's most popular restaurants, and it became known as a go-to place for breakfast meetings among Wichita's most prominent deal makers. Wong famously told the *Wichita Eagle* that he operated his restaurant under two tenets: treat people fairly and don't listen to their conversations. That drew in real estate kings like George Ablah and Dean Bussart, who would frequently breakfast with clients at Georgie Porgie, sometimes scratching out deals on napkins, said Ed Wong, Wayne's son, who worked in and eventually managed the restaurant.

"I probably put together more deals at Georgie Porgie's and Sambo's than I have in my own office," developer Ablah, who led the charge developing much of Wichita's east side, was quoted as saying in a 1981 story in the *Wichita Eagle-Beacon.*

The interior of the restaurant was no-frills, with a 1960s-era harvest gold color motif repeated in the flooring, on the wallpaper and on the booths and chairs. The menu offered an array of pancakes, from pecan to blueberry to cherry surprise, as well as omelets (the popular cheese omelet was just $2.95), waffles and corned beef hash. Breakfast was served all day, and buckwheat pancakes were a specialty. The lunch and dinner menu was populated with charbroiled steaks, meatloaf, fried chicken, burgers, ham salad sandwiches and fried seafood plates.

The Wongs sold Georgie Porgie's in 1990, but it operated until January 1998. Wayne's son, Ed, who still lives in Wichita, continued the family tradition, starting his own career in the Wichita restaurant industry. Among other ventures, he operated franchises of Spaghetti Jack's and Long John Silver's.

SWISS COLONY INN (1966)

In the mid-1960s, if Wichitans craved fondue, they could go to the Swiss Colony Inn, a combination cheese shop and restaurant at Twin Lakes Shopping Center. The restaurant was situated on the upper level in the southwestern-most building of the development, and it served gourmet sandwiches, salads and desserts. Fondue dinners were a popular evening feature.

In September 1971, a second Swiss Colony Inn opened at the southeast corner of the Garvey Center Kiva, which is the area below ground level that to this day is home to several businesses. The new restaurant had mostly the same menu as the Twin Lakes eatery, with the addition of an English breakfast buffet. The Garvey Center restaurant also featured a separate room with a "community table," where solo diners could sit with others while they ate. The interior had a Swiss-German theme, with a row of vinyl-covered booths bisecting the dining room and tables for two and six arranged around the perimeter. The décor was described by the *Wichita Beacon* as being quite in line with the looks and colors of the 1970s, with "arrangements of dried materials, whimsical wall groupings and hanging lamps over the booths and tables." Napkins and placemats were orange. Glassware was amber. And "translucent curtains in shades of rust" hung in the space.

The same year the Garvey Center restaurant was opened, Swiss Colony Inn's owners—Food Specialties Inc., which was a franchisee of the

Swiss Colony Inn had restaurants at Twin Lakes and downtown on the Garvey Center's ground level in the 1960s and 1970s. This picture was taken at the Twin Lakes restaurant in 1975. *From the* Wichita Eagle.

Wisconsin-based Swiss Colony cheese shop chain—announced plans to remodel the Twin Lakes restaurant and relocate its adjacent cheese shop to a different space in the center, on the lower level below Sears. Relocating the cheese shop allowed the restaurant to expand its capacity and add a waiting area. It also adopted some of the new items that had been introduced at the Garvey Center restaurant. Diners were reassured that the fondue dinners would also remain.

Fun fact: A sixteen-millimeter promotional film created in 1974 and titled *Wichita: Center City USA* features a brief glimpse of the Garvey Center restaurant and its sign. The film can be viewed at https://archive.org/details/WichitaCenterCityUSA.

It's unclear when exactly the two restaurants closed. The Twin Lakes cheese shop closed in 1981, and the following year, Food Specialties Inc. had a falling out with the Swiss Colony chain and changed the names of its two cheese shops still operating in Wichita—one at Towne East Square and one at Towne West Square—to Schimwitz Sausage & Cheese.

CASEY JONES JUNCTION (1968)

A generation of people who grew up in Wichita in the 1970s remembers that the greatest reward for good behavior or a stellar report card was a meal at Casey Jones Junction. The Acme Oil Corp., led by president and train enthusiast M. Eugene Torline, opened the first restaurant in 1968 at 3023 East Douglas, where Harry's Uptown is now. They had franchising plans in mind, and Torline visited the Casey Jones railroad museum in Jackson, Tennessee, to research the restaurant's namesake, a railroad folk hero who died in a train crash in 1900.

The company purchased and tore down an old Victorian home so they could build the first restaurant on the site. Inside, it featured a model train that

Top: Casey Jones Junction opened on East Douglas in 1968 and was built to resemble an old train depot. *Mark Funk.*

Bottom: Kids lucky enough to score a seat at the counter at Casey Jones Junction had their burgers and fries dropped off by a model train. *Mark Funk.*

The menu at Casey Jones Junction, which was founded by M. Eugene Torline and had two locations in Wichita. *Mark Funk.*

would choo choo "Tom Thumb" burgers to children seated at the counter. The menu also included chicken, charbroiled steaks and sandwiches, and it served breakfast. An advertisement in a 1969 edition of the *Catholic Advance* touted the restaurant's "sophisticated hamburgers and happy family foods." In addition to the train delivery system, the restaurant had a train theme throughout, and it was incorporated into the décor and menu.

Torline and his company franchised the restaurant, and in the early 1970s, there were eight restaurants, including in Dodge City and in Colorado. A second and larger Casey Jones Junction opened in 1970 at 6215 West Kellogg, where Lee's Chinese restaurant is now. In 1973, Torline acquired an eighty-five-foot antique railroad car that was said to have been used by the crown princess of Japan for her 1930 tour of the United States. The luxurious car had a parlor, dining room, kitchen, bath and bedroom, and its finishes were marble, stained glass and stainless steel. He parked it behind the restaurant and would often allow customers to tour it.

Casey Jones Junction closed when Torline died in 1986 at age sixty. His nephew, Mark Funk, who still lives in the Wichita area, has in his possession one of the model trains that delivered food at the west-side Casey Jones Junction.

1970-1979

Fern Bars, Supper Clubs and That Old English Flair

THOSE CRAZY LIQUOR LAWS, PART I

It's worth noting, as we launch into the 1970s, that the type of restaurants that opened and the way they operated were largely informed by liquor laws, and from the mid-1960s to the late 1980s, they were weird. But then, they have always been kind of weird.

Historically, Kansas has had a complicated relationship with alcohol. It is, after all, the home of the famous prohibitionist Carry Nation of Medicine Lodge, who, as a founder of the Woman's Christian Temperance Union in the late 1800s, was known for taking hatchets to the bars of establishments found to be flouting liquor laws. In 1900, she famously chopped up the bar at Wichita's Hotel Carey.

Kansas first passed prohibition laws in 1880, forty years before the rest of the country. And the state didn't repeal its prohibition legislation until 1948, fifteen years after it was repealed on a federal level. Even then, people could buy liquor only in state-licensed liquor stores, and a line was famously added to the state constitution that read, "The open saloon shall be and is hereby forever banned."

But the laws were widely ignored, and speakeasies and honky-tonks continued to operate fairly openly throughout the state. Eventually, clubs would illegally allow customers to bring in their own bottles of prepackaged wine and liquor and pay for a "set up" at the bar. These establishments were referred to as "bottle clubs."

The Private Club Act of 1965 was the state legislature's attempt to control bottle clubs and an illegal industry that was flourishing. The new rules allowed liquor by the drink at "private clubs," where people would have to pay a ten-dollar membership fee and wait ten days for their memberships to become valid before having a drink. That became the law of the land, but a 1979 act allowed restaurants with bars that earned at least 50 percent of their revenues from food to "reciprocate" membership lists with other restaurants serving liquor, making a membership card from one business good at hundreds of others across the state. Examples of "reciprocal clubs" in Wichita during this period were Crazy Horse Supper Club, Steak and Ale, Portobello Road, Scotch & Sirloin, The Hatch and Lakeshore Club.

Kansans got the chance in 1970 to approve another liquor by the drink measure, and although big counties like Sedgwick, Johnson, Wyandotte and Shawnee were in favor of the amendment, it failed 346,423 to 335,094 on the strength of the rural vote.

The status quo continued, but it was widely known to be a joke. Customers without membership cards could easily get into private clubs by borrowing a friend's card or pretending to know customers who had memberships. Most people agreed that the rules were a sham; people who wanted a drink could easily find ways to get one.

STEAK AND ALE (1970)

A few chain restaurants were loved enough by Wichita to demand inclusion on a list of long-lost favorites. One of them is Steak and Ale, a steakhouse chain that was founded by Norman E. Brinker in Dallas in 1966 and expanded across the country, opening a Wichita location at 8430 East Kellogg in 1970.

Steak and Ale restaurants were built to look like mid-seventeenth-century English inns, with stucco and timber on the exterior and stained glass, oak ceiling beams, wrought-iron chandeliers, deep carpet and fireplaces decorating the interior. Members of the staff even wore period costumes.

The restaurant was known not only for its steaks—the marinated Kensington Club was a top seller—but also for its first-rate salad bar. Almost all meals came with hot bread and unlimited access to the salad bar, which was stacked with chilled pewter salad plates.

For a time, the menus were printed onto actual meat cleavers with the title "Bill of Fare for Lords & Ladies" printed across the top. Other

Steak and Ale, a popular nationwide chain whose restaurants were designed to look like old English taverns, opened in Wichita in 1970. *Legendary Restaurant Brands.*

popular dishes on the menu were the Prince and Pauper, which was a meal that included both steak and marinated chicken; the Duke's Filet; a shish kabob called Beef on a Lance; and a steak and lobster dinner. The chain ran television commercials through the 1970s and 1980s that included a rousing ear-worm jingle: "Come sup with us at Steak and Ale, where hearty dining abounds."

Wichita's Steak and Ale was a popular draw for people celebrating birthdays and anniversaries and for teens headed to prom. It remained open until June 2000, and at the time, a manager told local media that the lease on the space was up and that with Kellogg expansion looming, the company decided not to renew. Another short-lived restaurant called The Chowder House Seafood and Lounge opened in the space in November of that year. By 2001, Mexican restaurant El Rodeo had moved in but had to vacate two years later when the building was targeted for demolition to make way for Kellogg construction. In 2008, all remaining Steak and Ale restaurants in the country closed when the chain went bankrupt. The company that now owns the Steak and Ale brand is Legendary Restaurant Brands, which is also the parent company for the Bennigan's chain. It recently launched a Steak and Ale comeback and is opening a new restaurant in Cancun, Mexico. As of 2021, the company was looking for U.S. franchisees.

BILL'S LE GOURMET (1970)

Bill Reaves loved jazz music. And the man could cook. In 1970, he combined his two passions and opened Bill's Le Gourmet, a seventy-seat restaurant and jazz club at 540 South Oliver.

For years, Reaves would attract a who's who crowd that would pack into the restaurant for his signature Steak Diane, which he served with a table-side preparation that always included a dramatic eruption of brandy-induced flames. The club was also known for its music. Reaves, who was one of the founders of the Wichita Jazz Festival and served as its president in 1976, was an accomplished pianist who would invite jazz musicians to his club for Sunday-night jam sessions. The sessions famously attracted not only local musicians but also jazz greats passing through town on their way to big city gigs—people like Oscar Peterson and Jay McShann. McShann's album *Man from Muskogee* was recorded at the club.

The house band was the Johnny Harris quartet, which was led by Harris—an original member of Ink Spots and a Billie Holiday musician. The quartet also included Art Hicks, Tommy Gray and Fred James, and it was a big draw.

Reaves grew up in Joplin, Missouri, and learned to cook from his mother. He opened his first nightclub there—called Ebony Club—when he was nineteen years old. In 1957, he moved to Wichita and took a job as a bellman at the Broadview Hotel, eventually working his way up to manager of the hotel's River Club. The affluent customers he met there followed him to his new restaurant, which thrived through the 1970s. But it closed in 1978, and his son—accomplished chef Anthony Card, who started his own restaurant career at age ten washing dishes at Bill's Le Gourmet—said his father was too willing to extend credit to his customers, and that's what did him in.

Reaves opened a second restaurant in 1980 at 2600 South Oliver. He called it French Quarter, but it lasted for only two years. He then took a job for a wholesale liquor distributor, but Reaves died in 1985 at age fifty-seven. His son, Card, has enjoyed a long restaurant career of his own, not only living and cooking for years in San Francisco but also leading kitchens at

Bill Reaves owned Bill's Le Gourmet at 540 South Oliver. It was a jazz club where Reaves was known to serve flaming Steak Diane tableside. *Anthony Card.*

Wichita institutions like Terradyne Country Club and Larkspur. He was also the chef and co-owner of a restaurant in the early 2000s called Restaurant 155 at 155 North Market.

DR. REDBIRD'S MEDICINAL INN (1971)

In the early 1970s, Rich Vliet was a young newlywed with a dream. He'd launched a career working with juvenile offenders but had always wanted to open a bar that served great sandwiches. When he married Marni Tasheff, a schoolteacher, in 1970, she became a partner in helping him achieve that dream. The Vliets, who would go on to open memorable Wichita restaurants like The Looking Glass and Larkspur, got their start in the restaurant business when they opened Dr. Redbird's Medicinal Inn in 1971.

It was at 124 South Main, across the street from Old City Hall, and the Vliets gave it an Old West medicine show theme, naming the restaurant for a cowboy outlaw known as Jesse Redbird. It was a full-service restaurant decorated with portraits of nineteenth-century politicians and Indian chiefs. The walls were brick, and the furniture was antique. Old church pews provided seating at some tables. The menus were printed on newsprint and used as placemats.

The Vliets developed the recipes for the restaurant's piled-high sandwiches, and they gave them names worthy of an Old West–style apothecary. Dr. Redbird's Daily Regulator was a top seller and featured hot ham and swiss cheese on an onion roll. The Supreme Preservative was an open-face sandwich made with wheatberry bread that was topped with sliced turkey breast and broccoli spears and covered with cheese sauce. In the early days, Dr. Redbird's sold a popular one-dollar lunch, which included a sandwich, chips, a kosher pickle and a choice of side—either wild rice with mushrooms, baked beans or potato salad made with Marni's mother's recipe. At the bar, customers could get pitchers of cold beer, and Dr. Redbird's also served cider—piping hot in the winter or ice cold in the summer.

The restaurant was instantly popular, and the Vliets went on to open four more Dr. Redbird's. The second one launched in 1972 at 4802 East Central, and in the following years, restaurants also were added at the Harry Street Mall, 3825 East Harry and Twin Lakes Shopping Center.

The Vliets had to move their original restaurant twice as buildings they were renting were sold. The first move was to 120 East Douglas, and the

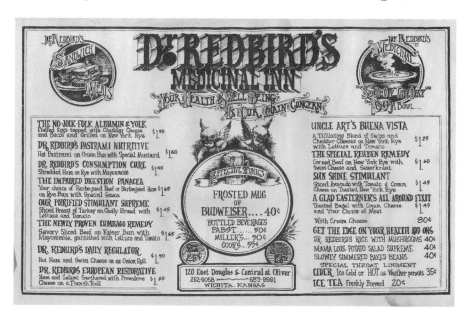

An early menu from Dr. Redbird's Medicinal Inn. *Marni Vliet Stone.*

second was across the street to 115 East Douglas. The last Dr. Redbird's to be added, which was a more upscale version of the originals, opened at Broadway Plaza, 2734 East Lincoln.

Over the years, sales at Dr. Redbird's started to sag as busy people opted to patronize drive-through chain sandwich shops rather than take the time for a sit-down experience. The Vliets turned two of their Dr. Redbird's—the ones at 115 East Douglas and at 4802 East Central—into barbecue restaurants called King Lizard. By 1985, they'd closed or sold the rest of the Redbird's restaurants. But Dr. Redbird's and its massive sandwiches live on in Wichitans' memories, as evidenced by the menus that still float around the internet and are frequently posted and reposted, even today.

ESTALITA'S TACOS (1971)

Estalita's Tacos, which operated in Wichita in the 1970s, 1980s and 1990s, is remembered not only for its burritos, tacos, enchiladas sanchos and "fire" hot sauce but also for its owner, Estalita "Little Esther" Smith, a Wichita native who was recognizable for her beehive hairdo and her blue eyeshadow. She and her husband, Tom, who was from Missouri but stationed at McConnell Air Force Base, opened the first Estalita's at 509 North Seneca in 1971 but had several others over the years, including at 139 North Broadway, at Central and Zoo, on South Meridian and finally at 2300 Southeast Boulevard. The Smiths' granddaughter Janell Smith remembered her grandfather grating huge blocks of cheese for the restaurant, which helped him develop his signature "Popeye" arms, and her grandparents always had large barrels full of beans soaking in the restaurant, which they'd later turn into refried beans. They steamed many of their menu items, which made the cheese melt just so, customers remember. "They kept their recipes very secret," Janell said. "I loved the smell of the food in the steamer."

Her grandparents worked six days a week, closing the restaurants only on Sundays, and they hired only family members. Janell said her mother worked there for more than five years when she was little, and Janell would sleep in a crib in the back. Her dad, Lendy, and his siblings Cindy and Tommy worked for the restaurant, too, and when Janell was a teen, she worked at the restaurant at Central and Zoo. Tommy also owned the Cowboy Club at the time.

In the restaurant, Esther wrote the receipts by hand and made hand-written signs she posted around the restaurant advertising her sauces, her

Taco Tuesday sale and other "quirky things," Janell said. Estalita's sold Choco Tacos for one dollar and always had a jar of ten-cent fireballs at the counter. The last Estalita's, at 2300 Southeast Boulevard, closed sometime in the mid-1990s. Tom Smith died in 2003, and Esther died in 2008.

KAMIEL'S RESTAURANT AND CLUB (1971)

Today, the name Shibley is associated in Wichita with heaping plates of biscuits and gravy at the popular Doo-Dah Diner, owned by Patrick and Timirie Shibley. But the first Shibley to make a mark on the local restaurant scene was Patrick Shibley's father, Kay. In 1971, he and partner Ted Christian opened Kamiel's Restaurant and Club in a new strip center built by developer Phil Ruffin at Kellogg and Rock Road. The business, whose address was 8065 Peachtree, served steaks, seafood and Lebanese specialties, and it was popular from opening day. An ad that ran in the *Wichita Eagle* just after the restaurant's opening weekend thanked the city for its acceptance, which the owners describe as "almost beyond our highest expectations. Sincere regrets for our inability to service some of the people who visited us this past weekend."

Just sixteen months later, a second Kamiel's opened at 2046 North West Street, and Shibley sent his young bartender Tom D'Annunzio and kitchen manager Sonny Glennon to run it. The pair bought it in 1972 and soon became known as the duo "Tom and Sonny," the eventual owners of Tom & Sonny's Supper Club at 3920 West Douglas, a club they opened after the west-side Kamiel's burned in a 1978 fire. D'Annunzio would go on to open Tommy's, which operated from 1992 to 2012 at Twenty-First and Tyler, and Glennon became a partner in Scotch & Sirloin.

Kamiel's East moved from its original spot to 6829 East Kellogg a few years after it opened, and Kay Shibley would launch many other food ventures over the years. In the late 1970s, he also briefly ran Kamiel's Family Restaurant at 7092 East Kellogg, which was known for its mulligan stew and chicken livers. He got out of the restaurant business for a short time in the late 1970s, and in 1977, he invented a salad topping he pitched as an alternative to croutons called Wheatons, made from pressure cooking wheat kernels. He got a partner and planned to market the product nationwide to restaurants with salad bars. (Patrick Shibley reports that Wheatons are still available at Wichita's Nifty Nut House.)

But the lure of the restaurant business was too strong, and in 1984, Kay Shibley opened another Kamiel's at 3117 East Douglas that served some of his customers' favorite dishes from his first go-round, things like broiled chicken breast, broiled steak with mushroom sauce and Lebanese specialties like cabbage rolls, grape leaves and kibbeh balls. That restaurant lasted until 1990, and in 2005, he made a brief return to open a restaurant called Krazy Kaz at 3407 East Douglas, where College Hill Deli is now. It had been fifteen years, but he was "tired of sitting around," he told the *Wichita Eagle* when he opened the restaurant.

Kay Shibley died in 2007, but his restaurant legacy continues at Doo-Dah Diner, 206 East Kellogg, where son Patrick has hung the first Kamiel's menu in a place of honor on a wall.

THE OLD WAY STATION (1973)

The cover of the menu from the Old Way Station, a popular restaurant in 1970s Wichita. There was also a stained-glass window in the restaurant with this design. *Jeanne Johnson-Bennett.*

In 1973, seasoned restaurateur Jim Aboud announced plans to open a new club and restaurant in a former antique store at 6615 East Central. The Old Way Station was somewhat hidden, accessible only off an alleyway, but those who found it were greeted by a brick building full of antiques, stained glass and even a salad bar made out of the old Miller Theatre ticket booth.

Aboud was already a player on the Wichita restaurant scene, having started Flaming Steer steakhouses and operated Mr. Steak in the late 1960s. His new 275-person club and restaurant had a Tudor motif, and the interior was designed with plank flooring and furnishings that harkened back to old English taverns. There was a wooden bar situated in the middle of the main room, and customers could sit in floor-to-ceiling booths and walk on maroon flowered carpet. The building also contained a famous "library room" that included a wood-burning stone fireplace that was reportedly imported from a castle in Switzerland.

Aboud described the club upon its opening as an informal eating and drinking place that served sandwiches, soups, omelets, full-course dinners, wine and exotic drinks. The menu listed dishes like eggs Benedict, shrimp boiled in beer and filet of lemon sole. There were also burgers, prime rib, seafood platters, catfish and steak and lobster plates. The salad bar had fifteen items, including a giant block of cheese that customers could shave pieces off of and a spaghetti bar that offered four different types of sauces. The club also had live piano and organ music and would occasionally project old movies for its customers' enjoyment. Many Wichitans remember having bridal showers and wedding luncheons at the club, which also served brunch.

The Old Way Station, which in 1973 was forced to remove a forty-foot sign after the City of Wichita determined it was an eyesore, appears to have closed around 1982. In 1985, Alan Bundy opened an Amarillo Grill restaurant in the space. Today, it's home to a dance studio. Aboud died in 2011.

PORTOBELLO ROAD (1973)

During the 1970s and 1980s, one of Wichita's most stylish, classy restaurants was Portobello Road. In August 1973, it took over the building at 504 South Bluff where onetime favorite Elizabeth's had operated until the late 1960s. To find the entrance, customers had to walk down a secluded passageway between two buildings, and when they opened the door, they were greeted by an Old English–style dining room created by famed Wichita interior designer Burton Pell. It featured dark wood, brick wall accents, a fireplace and deep-red chairs. Several small rooms made up the restaurant, which featured lantern ceiling fixtures and lots of antique brass, copper, pewter and wrought-iron touches.

Portobello Road opened as a public restaurant and private club, and its owners were businessmen Larry Frasco, Bill Lusk Jr. and Mike Osterhout. The owners said at the time that they wanted the décor to feature the look of pubs on stylish Portobello Road in London's Kensington District. About one hundred diners could fit inside the restaurant, where they could choose from items like prime rib, steak, beef rolls, chicken in wine sauce and trout almandine. A specialty of the house was the Round Table Royale, a dish that included meat, fish and fowl and was served with rice pilaf.

"The management will act in continental style, presenting female guests with a flower and men with a cigar," read a *Wichita Eagle and Beacon* article printed when Portobello Road first opened. There was a big hubbub in

Portobello Road was one of Wichita's most stylish restaurants during the 1970s and 1980s.
From the Wichita Eagle.

1978, when Wichita's Urban Renewal Agency renovated the old Rock
Island Depot at 711 East Douglas and chose Portobello Road to get the lease
to operate there. The agency and the restaurant went back and forth over
who should pay for an elevator to transport patrons with disabilities from the
downstairs restaurant to an upstairs disco, but it was all moot in the end. At
the last minute, Frasco was unable to secure the money to make the move
and pulled out of the deal.

Portobello Road continued on, though, and by the 1980s, the restaurant
was considered one of Wichita's finest. Many local couples got engaged
there over dinner. In 1980, Frasco said he had the best wine list in the state,
and his menu was full of upscale dishes like Cornish game hen stuffed with
wild rice, Alaskan king crab, fresh Maine lobster, escargot and oysters on the
half shell. When Frasco died in 1993, his widow, Jill, put the restaurant up
for sale and then closed it on New Year's Eve. But she soon found buyers in
former regulars Bob and Marlys Kretchmar, who took over and reopened
the restaurant in early 1994, hiring a new chef and updating the restaurant's
lighting. In 1996, the Kretchmars learned they'd be losing the space that held
Portobello Road, which was set to be demolished to make way for Kellogg
expansion. In an interesting turn, the Kretchmars decided to move the
restaurant to the Rock Island Depot building where it had nearly relocated
almost twenty years earlier. The restaurant reopened there with seating for
165 in November 1996. Three years later, though, Portobello Road reached
the end of its road. The Kretchmars closed it at the end of 1999.

LA PALMA (1974)

Another famous resident of the Wishbone Building at 5231 East Central was La Palma, a Mexican restaurant owned by German Reyes and run with the help of his family. La Palma moved into the oddly shaped building with a wishbone-shaped roofline in 1979, taking over the space after the popular Fife and Drum vacated it. Reyes, who had previously run La Palma for five years at Lincoln and Governeour, was a native of Bogotá, Colombia. He was trained as an engineer but got into the restaurant business with the help of his Colombian-born wife, Fabiola, who ran the front of the restaurant. La Palma was known for serving hot tortillas with butter, and its menu was also full of items like fresh tamales, pork chile verde, ham flautas, huevos rancheros and chili rellenos.

Reyes was also fascinated by the history of the Wishbone Building, and its storied past—which included an early run as a speakeasy during Prohibition—was recounted on the placemats. But by 1992, Reyes had decided that the space, where he could seat only eighty-six diners, was too small for him to turn a profit. He told the *Wichita Eagle* at the time he would consider reopening in a bigger spot and targeted the growing Twenty-Ninth and Rock Road area as his ideal location, but that never happened. Jet Bar-B-Q then took over the Wishbone Building.

MR. DUNDERBAK'S (1975)

Wichita got a new mall—Towne East Square—in 1975, and one of its original tenants was Mr. Dunderbak's Bavarian Pantry, which opened on the upper level closest to the former Sear's spot. The owner was Rose Kuhlman, known in Wichita for opening Scotch & Sirloin with her husband, Delmar. She'd franchised the chain, based in Cherryhill, New Jersey, and opened its sixteenth store, which at the time would have been the chain's largest and the only one within about one thousand miles of Wichita. The menu would specialize in "fast-food delicatessen items," according to an article in the *Wichita Beacon*, and they would be made with imported meats and cheeses. Beer was also to be served.

The long, skinny restaurant was fashioned to look like an old German meat market, and polka music was usually playing in the background. Customers who entered could see into a walk-in cooler displaying all the meats and cheeses, and employees were costumed "in the Bavarian manner," according to the *Wichita Beacon*. Visitors could choose to sit at the counter that stretched the length of the restaurant or take a seat at one of the tables in the back. *Wichita Beacon* food columnist Kathleen Kelly reviewed the restaurant in 1976 and had good things to say about her meal, which was the special of the day and cost her $1.95. It included fried kielbasa with kraut and German-style potato salad, a thick slice of seedy rye bread and a drink. Kelly noted that the restaurant also served sandwiches like roast beef, corned beef, kassler liverwurst and Reubens as well as sausages, German wieners, sauerkraut, pickles and desserts like strudel. Visitors also could shop from an assortment of smoked sausages, imported cheese and other food items from around the world. A waitress told Kelly that there were several Germans working in the Wichita store, but "because I didn't hear any foreign accents, I expect she had in mind Americans of German descent," Kelly wrote.

Mr. Dunderbak's was a popular draw to Towne East Square for more than a decade, but in 1987, the mall launched a major remodel that included the addition of a food court almost right outside Mr. Dunderbak's front door. Owner Kuhlman said she wasn't up for the competition and moved the restaurant out of the mall and to a spot at Kellogg and Woodlawn, changing the name to Mr. Dunderbak's Old World Cafe and Delicatessen. In an ad placed in the *Wichita Eagle* that year, the new restaurant was described as carrying the same wurst and kraut it had served in the mall but with the addition of "more traditional German cuisine, imported beers, wines and even cocktails." Among the authentic dishes the new Dunderbak's would carry, the ad promised: wiener schnitzel, roulade, sauerbraten, kasseler rippchen and even red cabbage and German dumplings. The relocated restaurant was also to offer German ballads, marching songs and polkas and be decorated with an "Old World" look. But the relocated restaurant closed about a year later, and Kuhlman went on to concentrate on a new healthy-dining restaurant she'd opened called Gourmet 500.

Mr. Dunderbak's is one of those restaurants that Wichitans still frequently talk about today. Many had their first jobs there, and others are still dreaming about its sandwiches, its kraut dogs and the delicious smells that would waft from the restaurant into the corridors of the mall.

DIAMOND HEAD (1975)

In the mid-1970s, Wichita diners were treated to something new: a taste of Polynesia. Hong Kong native David Y.W. Lau and his partners, who also had five restaurants on the East Coast—including the exotic-sounding Royal Hawaiian Supper Club in Washington, D.C.—in 1975 opened Diamond Head on the lower level of Seneca Square Shopping Center, Thirty-First Street South and Seneca. The restaurant took over a space that had previously been occupied by the Empress Chinese Restaurant.

On the menu was Polynesian fare like flaming pu pu platters and drinks like Mai Tais. The menu also offered Chinese food, including popular dishes like sweet and sour chicken. A separate Luau Room was available for private parties.

"We want to have the number one restaurant in the whole town," Lau told the *Wichita Eagle* shortly after Diamond Head opened. "We didn't come 1,000 miles just to open a chop suey house."

People who remember Diamond Head say it had atmosphere to spare, including booths under thatched tiki huts and drinks decorated with tiny umbrellas. It was dark inside, and the service was impeccable. If you even got a cigarette out of your purse or jacket, a manager was immediately at your side with a lighter.

By 1986, the restaurant was owned by Joe and Judy Cheng, who announced plans to move it to a new building at 5825 West Central. The brick restaurant was to have six thousand square feet of space and a special club area. Diamond Head moved, and customers followed, but many say it was never the same. Diamond Head lasted on West Central until 1998. Today, the space is occupied by the China Star Super Buffet.

APPLEGATE'S LANDING (1975)

It used to be that Pizza Hut International would occasionally try spinoff concepts. One of them was Applegate's Landing, which launched in Wichita in 1975, the brainchild of executives Keith Hansen and Ed Elpers. The two were hoping to attract middle-class customers with children, and they wanted to open restaurants in existing structures they could refurbish. The first Applegate's Landing was at 1343 North Oliver, and more followed over the next several years: Towne East Square in 1975, 1415 West Pawnee in 1977 and 3020 West Thirteenth Street in 1978.

Applegate's Landing focused on pizza, but the recipe was different from Pizza Hut's. These pies were made with thick Sicilian or crispy Italian-style crusts. Sub sandwiches and pasta were also on the menu, and people today still drool over the memory of Applegate's Landing's Gilbertini pasta, made with Italian sausage, cheddar, mozzarella and garlic. The restaurants also offered big salad bars, which in many locations were set up in the back of antique trucks. In later years, prime rib was added to the menu.

The restaurants' designs were also unique. The exteriors featured shake shingles and stone river rock that made the structures look like Colonial-style houses. The interiors had brickwork and oak flooring, and the design had many memorable features, including four-foot-high doors that kids loved, booths with their own lighting setups that could be controlled by customers, stained glass and a private brick silo that could accommodate large groups. Some tables were lined with old tractor seats for chairs. People could also sit on porch swings or in garden gazebos. A 1975 article in the *Wichita Eagle and Beacon* described the waitresses as being "appropriately costumed in long granny dresses, bandana dresses and girl-fashioned bib overalls."

By 1980, there were twenty-two Applegate's Landing restaurants in eleven states. But that year, Pizza Hut sold its Applegate's Landing division to Wichita-based Wurth Corporation, which announced plans to continue developing the chain. Elpers was tapped to head operations, having quit Pizza Hut six months earlier to negotiate an Applegate's Landing purchase. In 1982, the Towne East restaurant was renamed Von's, and it added homemade pie to the menu. But a few months later, Von's and the three remaining Applegate's Landing restaurants closed "because they were not meeting financial expectations," according to a story in the *Wichita Eagle and Beacon*. Applegate's Landing restaurants in other cities continued to operate for a while, and in 1995, the last restaurant in the chain, which was at First and Mulberry in McPherson, closed its doors. A dentist's office took it over, and the building still resembles from the outside the Applegate's Landing look of old.

Applegate's Landing was a popular Pizza Hut spinoff that launched in Wichita in 1975. *From the* Wichita Eagle.

THE LOOKING GLASS (1975)

In the mid-1970s, Rich and Marni Vliet were among Wichita's most prominent restaurateurs and the owners of the popular Dr. Redbird's Medicinal Inn restaurants. In 1975, they opened The Looking Glass, a private club that the *Wichita Eagle*'s Diane Lewis called Wichita's "first fern bar," a slang term used at the time to describe upscale bars decorated with live plants and that appealed to young singles.

In 1973, the couple had taken over and started remodeling the historic Mead Building, which was built in 1915 at 412 East Douglas and had previously held White Way Recreation—a deteriorating pool hall, restaurant and bar that attracted an unsavory crowd. Eight months into the remodel, though, fire broke out in the building and the Vliets had to start all over. But they were finally able to open The Looking Glass in January 1975, and Wichita was wowed by what they'd achieved.

The Looking Glass interior was filled with hanging plants and natural wood finishes. It was decorated with antique mirrors, rust-colored banquettes, bentwood chairs, a tin ceiling and collectible light fixtures suspended from the ceiling. The most stunning addition was a massive stained-glass dome that had been a part of the First Methodist Church in Arkansas City; the Vliets purchased it at a 1973 auction for $300. They installed it over The Creperie, which was the club's public restaurant. There was a separate private dining area as well as a bar area that featured the White Way's old bar and backbar "restored to their original magnificence," according to the *Wichita Eagle*. The Creperie, staffed by a Dodge City native who had trained in France, offered a menu of salads, soups, entrée crepes and dessert crepes. In the private club dining area, the lunch menu offered Danish, French, Mediterranean and American sandwiches, and at dinner, it served entrées like beef burgundy and Oysters Rockefeller.

The Looking Glass was a Wichita favorite for nearly a decade and a popular hangout for journalists from the nearby *Wichita Eagle*. But at the start of 1984, the Vliets put the business on the market as they eyed other development opportunities. The Looking Glass closed in March 1985, and the Vliets converted the space into offices. In recent years, the Looking Glass space has been home to art galleries, and the upstairs has for years been home to cabaret theater—first Cabaret Old Town and now Roxy's Downtown.

In the late 1980s, Rich Vliet formed Marketplace Properties with architect Dave Burk, and the company was key in developing Wichita's Old Town entertainment district. In 1992, he and Burk opened one of Old Town's first

Left: Rich and Marni Vliet took over the historic Mead building at 412 East Douglas and turned it into the popular 1970s fern bar The Looking Glass. *Marni Vliet Stone*.

Below: The lobby of The Looking Glass, which operated from 1975 to 1985. *Marni Vliet Stone*.

The Looking Glass was decorated with live plants, antique mirrors and a tin ceiling. *Marni Vliet Stone.*

restaurants, Larkspur, at 904 East Douglas. They sold it a few years later, though it's still in operation today.

Rich Vliet died in 2011 after a nine-year battle with ALS. Marni donated the famous stained-glass dome that once decorated The Looking Glass to Botanica, where Rich Vliet had once served as chairman of the board. It now hangs over the entry hall to Botanica's event center.

JUDGE RIGGS (1975)

One of Wichita's hottest tickets in the mid-1970s was Judge Riggs, a restaurant and nightclub that operated inside the Hilton Inn East hotel at Kellogg and Rock Road. The club opened in the summer of 1975, as did a separate restaurant called Ziggies, a month before the $6 million hotel. The instantly popular club was named after Wichita's first judge, Reuben Riggs. It was a private club, though portions of the dining room were open to the public, and it was known for its singing wait staff (though it was nearly impossible in the early days to get a reservation to be served by the singing staff.)

Judge Riggs also was known as an expensive place to dine. According to *Wichita Beacon* food writer Kathleen Kelly, though, it was worth it. In a review of Judge Riggs she published in 1976, Kelly praised the restaurant's quality and hoped that the hype that surrounded its opening wouldn't fade away. "The prices are 'big city' and may frighten some. But the food is so excellent and the surroundings so delightful that it's well worth the tab," she wrote.

The menu included fancy entrées like barbecued crab, London broil, Cornish game hen and prime rib. Diners could get sourdough cheese bread, a house specialty, as an appetizer, as well as escargot, herring in cream and shrimp cocktail. The dessert menu included 1970s hits like peach melba and baked Alaska. Kelly, who was impressed when a waitress brought a finger bowl with lemon and extra napkins so she could clean up after a feast of crab, hoped Wichitans wouldn't be too scandalized by the price of the twin lobster tails: $14.95. "But for the price, one also gets the engaging and professional entertainment provided by those who serve you," Kelly wrote.

The club was the place to be for years. The year after it opened, it was often filled to capacity, even on weeknights as "many young adults and some nearing middle aged" crowded in to hear dance bands and other live acts, according to the *Wichita Beacon*. The party would last until 3:00 a.m. Judge Riggs was gone by 1984, and a new club moved into the space.

Judge Riggs was a popular restaurant and nightclub known for its singing wait staff. This photo was taken in 1975. *From the* Wichita Eagle.

ICHIBAN (1976)

Etsuko Meeks opened the tiny Japanese restaurant Ichiban in 1976. This ad appeared in the *Wichita Eagle* on April 10, 1976.

Ichiban was a tiny Japanese restaurant that opened in 1976 at 1002 South Seneca. It lasted until 1992 and is one of the restaurants most mentioned when locals list their onetime favorites.

Owned by Tokyo native Etsuko Meeks, the restaurant operated out of a small building that could seat only about forty-five diners at once. One side of the dining room held a row of booths. The other side was furnished with low tables and cushions, the kind that diners would find in an authentic Japanese teahouse. The waitresses wore kimonos.

Meeks, who staffed the kitchen herself, offered several different Japanese-style dinners that would include things like soup dotted with tofu and lemon peel, sukiyaki cooked tableside in a cast-iron skillet and tempura. Diners could also order teriyaki and a Japanese rice bowl dish known as donburi, and they could get sashimi. Those with less adventurous palates could order steak, crab—even a burger and fries.

The restaurant closed in 1992, and the building was eventually home to another favorite Wichita eatery—The Breakfast Club. The space held a series of eateries over the years and is still operating as a restaurant today. Friends of Meeks say she went on to staff the sushi counter at a local Dillons store. She died in 2000 at age seventy-six.

R&S BAR-B-Q (1976)

One of Charles Ray's four children was working at Adams Barbecue when its founder, Jerome Adams, died unexpectedly in 1970. Charles was asked to step in and manage the place, and because he had four kids to put through college, he agreed. Ray kept it going until 1976, when another couple took it over, and he and his wife, Hattie, opened their own restaurant in an aluminum-sided building at 1918 East Thirteenth Street. It had seating for sixty and drew an eclectic crowd of people, from businessmen on lunch breaks to neighborhood residents to students from nearby Wichita State University. Fans would frequently arrive to find a line stretched around the building as people waited their turn to have Charles hand them paper plates

Hattie and Charles Ray, longtime owners of R&S Bar-B-Q, are pictured here in their restaurant, *second and third from left*, in 1992 with the two couples who bought the business. *From the* Wichita Eagle.

filled with a heaping pile of ribs or brisket or hot links plus bread and pickles on the side. Hattie served drinks and operated the cash register.

R&S remained popular through the 1990s, but the couple steadily decreased the hours as the years went on. In 1992, the restaurant was open only from 11:00 a.m. to 3:00 p.m. on Thursdays and Fridays. Three years later—in 1996—Charles and Hattie sold the restaurant to new owners. R&S lasted until 2001.

GATSBY'S (1977)

Jeanne and Floyd Ellis were the founders of Gatsby's, which years after it was gone was referred to in the *Wichita Eagle* as a "swanky supper club." At the time, Floyd Ellis, a World War II veteran, was considered a seasoned businessman, having already opened places like The Cypress, a club he started in 1954; the Stardust; and Steak Ranch. Floyd married Jeanne, and five years later, in 1977, they opened Gatsby's at 7152 East Kellogg. In 1980, Floyd told the *Wichita Beacon* that his goal was "to bring Wichita an elegant place serving fine food," a place where "people can go out and dress up." The Ellises said they were going for the feel of a speakeasy from the 1920s, and they decorated the inside with mirrored walls, heavy draperies that could be positioned to make booths private, wicker furniture and lots of potted plants. The space was divided into two separate areas: a more formal dining room with seating for eighty and a lounge with seating for sixty that also had a small corner dance floor and offered "low-key" live entertainment.

Gatsby's was where people would go for romantic nights out or special occasion meals. The menu was upscale and pricey for the times, and it offered dishes like Veal Gatsby, featuring veal strips sautéed in butter and topped with crab meat, mushrooms, asparagus and béchamel sauce. There were also steak and seafood dishes, a large wine list and a bartender who liked to use ice cream in decadent drinks like Tumbleweeds and Brandy Ices. In 1987, the Ellises embarked on a $150,000 remodel and expansion of the club, which added one thousand square feet and a solid brass wine dispenser that let customers order sixteen different wines by the glass. Gatsby's lasted until 1989, when the Ellises sold the restaurant to Barbara and Mark Sun, who at the time owned Imperial Palace Chinese restaurant at 303 East Pawnee. The Suns renamed the restaurant Mandarin. Tragedy struck five years later when four masked men entered Mandarin, robbed it and fatally shot Barbara Sun, who was just thirty-five.

LETTUCE CLUB (1977)

No one really remembers the food at Lettuce Club—although it did have a kitchen that put out "exotic" burgers, shredded beef sandwiches and veggie trays. It also had a salad bar stocked, presumably, with lettuce.

But it was one of Wichita's more colorful establishments, which locals still (hazily) remember and reminisce about to this day. It was opened in 1977 at 458 North Waco by Lee Aronfeld and some partners. Aronfeld was the president of the LeMans arcade chain at the time. Lettuce took over a 1916 building that had in its early life held a grocery store. The interior was long and narrow but was remodeled to offer 4,000 square feet of floor space that included multiple levels and a 105-foot bar, said to be the longest in the state at the time. The dance floor, which of course was set up under a disco ball, had a parallelogram shape and was surrounded by bleachers.

The club was a hit with young singles ages twenty-one to thirty, who would pack it every weekend night. Often, people would stand in lines to get in that wrapped around the building. And that line was no doubt filled with people eager to get started on the club's "three-for-one" drink special or to try one of its famous cocktail concoctions like Lettuceade or the Chocolate Snow Bear.

Lettuce was more of a nightclub than a restaurant, but it was a huge part of the singles scene in 1970s and 1980s Wichita. *From the* Wichita Eagle.

Lettuce was unapologetic about its status as a pick-up joint. Its matchbooks, when opened, were filled with blank spaces for "name, address and phone" followed by the words "You met me at Lettuce." The club would put on some pretty crazy events, including a "Dating Game" contest, a version of "The Gong Show" and shows featuring male strippers. There was roller disco on Sundays and belly dancers and magicians on other nights. The bartenders were performers who would spin drink cups and stage water fights. There was a dress code, and jeans were not allowed unless the guys working the door deemed them "high fashion."

Lettuce was a popular hangout for Wichita Wings fans and players, who would meet there after games. Patrons remember that the band Dire Straits once performed there. Others say members of Bon Jovi once showed up. Lettuce lasted through the early 1980s, but mentions of it stopped appearing in the newspaper by 1986.

THE HATCH COVER (1978)

It was best known to modern-day diners as Kwan Court. But the building at 1443 North Rock Road that held the famous Chinese restaurant from 1990 until 2011 was one of the hippest clubs in town for a brief span that started in the late 1970s and ended in the mid-1980s. Called The Hatch Cover, or more commonly The Hatch, the private club opened on Halloween 1978 and was designed to look like a Colorado getaway, with lots of natural wood accents, high ceilings, a copper fireplace, big windows and ferns everywhere. The bar area was a particularly popular hangout, and the young and hip would crowd into the area, leaning against the bar railing when there were no seats available, which was frequently. Many would migrate over from the Racquet Club next door, still wearing their tennis clothes, and would listen to live music as they socialized over margaritas, pina coladas and fruit daiquiris or snacked on fried zucchini strips or lavash crackers topped with melted cheese. The Hatch was open for lunch and dinner, and the kitchen invented some interesting dishes.

The Hatch Cover was one of Wichita's hippest hangouts in the late 1970s and early 1980s. It operated in the space on Rock Road that would later hold Kwan Court. *From the Wichita Eagle.*

The lunch menu had an item called the Persnickety Saladwich, built on homemade pumpernickel bread and topped with avocado, Monterey Jack cheese and crab salad. Another popular noontime dish featured walnut-studded chicken salad piled on top of a slice of cantaloupe. The dinner menu featured a steak and enchilada dinner as well as a filet medallion topped with crab meat, artichoke hearts and béarnaise.

In 1985, Charley Brown—the son of Brown's Grill founder Richard Brown—took over the space and reopened it as Charley Brown's Restaurant & Lounge. It closed in 1987, and three years later, Kwan Court moved in.

TOM & SONNY'S CLUB (1978)

Tom D'Annunzio and Sonny Glennon were old friends and business partners, having run a popular restaurant and club called Kamiel's II at Twenty-First and West in the early 1970s. But after a fire gutted the restaurant in 1978, the friends decided to go into business together and opened Tom & Sonny's in a space at 3920 West Douglas that had once held a Safeway. A photo that accompanied an ad for the new restaurant showed the two friends standing under the sign at their new club, both mustached with large-collared shirts and floppy hair. The ad promised a "beautiful new club" that would seat 350 and offer live entertainment five nights a week. The menu would consist of steak, seafood and Lebanese fare. Tom & Sonny's became one of Wichita's most popular restaurants through the 1980s and was known for its personal service, excellent prime rib and big salad bar. It was the site of many special occasion dinners and raucous office Christmas parties.

D'Annunzio sold his interest in the club to Glennon in 1986—just one year before liquor-by-the-drink passed and gave the restaurant a boost. Glennon held on until 1989, when the restaurant declared bankruptcy as business dried up. By the end of that year, a new restaurant called Italian Garden was operating in the space. By 1990, Glennon had taken over as general manager at Scotch & Sirloin, eventually becoming a partner with Lindy Andeel and Doug Farha. That restaurant is still open, though its current owner, Mike Issa, bought it in 2014.

D'Annunzio and his wife, Judy, opened a new club called Tommy's at Twenty-First and Tyler in 1992. It was a hotspot for dining and dancing in its day, but it closed in 2012.

OLIVE TREE (1979)

Perhaps the most influential figure on the modern Wichita restaurant scene was Antoine Toubia, an immigrant from Beirut, Lebanon, who started his restaurant empire in 1979. Many current-day restaurant owners got their starts in one of Toubia's many establishments, and local chefs credit him with introducing a new style of cuisine to a "meat and potatoes" town. Toubia, who grew up with a mother who excelled at cooking, attended culinary school in Beirut and moved to the United States in 1970, settling first in New York City and then relocating to Kansas City in 1972. He arrived in Wichita in 1973 and was hired as a chef at Wichita's Crestview Country Club, where he impressed local diners with his appreciation for ethnic fare as well as for sauces and proteins other than chicken and steak.

In 1979, he opened his first restaurant—the Olive Tree—in a modest log cabin–shaped building at 540 South Oliver that had previously housed Bill's Le Gourmet. There, he introduced Wichita to things like quiche, crepes and hummus and dishes made with fresh garlic and plain yogurt, ingredients Toubia had a hard time even finding in Wichita. His empire grew from there, and by the time of his premature death from cancer of the esophagus at age forty-seven in 1996, Toubia was the head of a food service company called Latour that included several restaurants and big food service contracts.

Over the years, Toubia was responsible not only for the Olive Tree but also for restaurants like Cafe Chantilly, Sac Souk, Piccadilly Grill, Bagatelle Bakery and more.

But the Olive Tree was always his flagship. It moved twice: first in 1980 to 7335 East Kellogg after a fire destroyed his original building, and then in 1987 to a large and luxurious space at Twenty-Ninth and Rock Road. The new space had room for a sister restaurant next door, which would also become popular: Chelsea's Bar & Grill. It also had a large banquet space. During Olive Tree's long tenure, it developed a reputation as one of Wichita's finest restaurants. It served Mediterranean and continental cuisine with entrées like hazelnut-crusted red snapper, veal loin and herb-crusted lamb loin. Toubia

Antoine Toubia, the founder of the Latour restaurant group, had a major influence on Wichita's restaurant scene. He's pictured here in 1984. *From the Wichita Eagle.*

entrusted Olive Tree's operation to his sisters, Joumana and Randa. Both the Olive Tree and Chelsea's remained popular for two decades. Toubia's siblings, helped for a time by his sons, took over running his company after his death. But the Olive Tree and Chelsea's were evicted from the space at Twenty-Ninth and Rock in 2009 after a dispute with the landlord.

The siblings managed to reclaim the space seven years later, in 2016, and once again ran its banquet hall as well as a new restaurant in the former Chelsea's spot, which they called Two Olives. It's still open as of this writing.

THE GRAPE (1979)

Mark Silverman, a New York native who'd been bartending in Traverse City, Michigan, moved to Wichita in 1978 for one reason: He wanted to open a wine bar. His father, a salesman, had told him Wichita was a good market, and Silverman found a two-story space in Mill Creek Village, a strip center at 550 North Rock Road, where he built his new business, The Grape. It opened in October 1979 and was said to be Wichita's first wine bar. Silverman stocked fifty-five wines, selling thirty by the glass, as well as sixteen imported beers. He served alcohol, too, but only one brand of each spirit. Wine and beer were his focus.

It was a sophisticated business that featured seating for 110. It was furnished with comfortable red chairs and decorated with six hundred wine bottles hanging from the rafters. Silverman added little touches that gave the place atmosphere, like a news rack stocked with the *Wichita Eagle Beacon* as well as the *New York Times* and the *Wall Street Journal.* He played jazz and classical music quietly in the background and served a small menu that consisted of a quiche of the day, a few salads and a large selection of deli sandwiches, made with meat and cheese cut at the deli counter tucked in the corner. Silverman's bar became even more popular in the summer of 1982, when he added an outdoor upper-level deck with 36 seats, making The Grape the first restaurant in town where food was served outdoors. Patrons loved sitting on the deck and catching a summer breeze. The menu was expanded, and by 1985, diners could also get skewered escargot, cheese boards, salads, fried shrimp with pasta and appetizers like fried mushrooms, potato skins and shrimp cocktail. The Grape was open late, and it became a favorite place for people to gather after a show.

But in 1990, it suddenly closed, and customers soon learned that Silverman had sold his business to new owners Jim Bachman and Tom Carson, two

Mark Silverman opened Wichita's first wine bar, The Grape, in 1979. *From the* Wichita Eagle.

men who had both worked for Latour restaurant group. They freshened up the place and reopened it with a new bistro menu that featured burgers, pizza, steaks, seafood dishes, omelets and pasta. Diane Lewis, the *Wichita Eagle*'s restaurant writer at the time, had been a longtime customer of The Grape and said she liked the change, writing in 1990 that "the new Grape still has the charm of the old but there's even more to be charmed by now."

The Grape remained a popular destination through the 1990s, but Bachman sold it in 2002, and by 2003, it had closed. The new owners opened a restaurant and club in the space called The Shadow, and a series of other businesses have operated there over the years, including a fine dining restaurant and a dueling piano bar. As of this writing, it's home to a restaurant called Crutch BBQ.

1980-1989

Fine Dining, Fun Dining and the Early Days of Old Town

GRANDY'S (1980)

It's safe to say that Wichita will never get over the loss of Grandy's, which operated in town from 1980 to 1999. Years later, locals are still wistfully wishing for—and sometimes publicly lobbying for—its return. Grandy's Country Cupboard, a fast-food chicken chain founded in Lewisville, Texas, in 1972, announced in 1979 that it was entering the Wichita market with a menu focused on country fried chicken, chicken fried steak dinners, homemade yeast rolls, mashed potatoes and country cream gravy, baked beans and coleslaw. The first two Wichita restaurants opened in 1980 at 233 South West Street and 4222 East Harry.

The next two were open by 1981 at 2347 South Seneca and 8303 East Kellogg, followed by 8320 West Central in 1986 and 2241 North Woodlawn in 1988. The restaurants featured drive-throughs and gave many Wichita kids their first jobs. Wichitans loved the restaurant's affordable food and were particularly crazy for its baked items, especially the fluffy dinner rolls and gooey cinnamon rolls. Grandy's sales started to decline over the 1990s, and in August 1999, the company closed its restaurants in Wichita citing "unsatisfactory financial results." Wichita has been in mourning ever since.

The chain still exists, though it's now based in Nashville, and it has forty-five locations in Texas, Oklahoma, New Mexico, Tennessee, Kentucky, Georgia and Indiana. Every few years, rumors start to swirl that Grandy's is coming back to Wichita. And every few years, someone starts a social media campaign to try to persuade the company that it's a good idea. Grandy's spokespeople have said in recent years they're not opposed to the idea. But so far, there's been no movement.

CHI CHI'S (1980)

When the first Wichita Chi Chi's opened in May 1980 at 6160 East Central, the Louisville-based Mexican restaurant chain was only three years old. But Mike Kelly, a former Wichitan who had built more than five hundred Pizza Hut restaurants, and his partner Joe Johnston had opened a Chi Chi's in Oklahoma City and were about to expand into Tulsa and Overland Park. They guessed, correctly, that Wichita would love it, too. Wichita's new Chi Chi's promised affordable Mexican dishes like chimichangas and nachos and the best margaritas in town, and locals went especially crazy for the restaurant's happy hour. Wichita's Chi Chi's was so busy that a manager told the *Wichita Eagle* in 1982 that sales were surpassing the $2.2 million yearly average for the chain. A second restaurant opened two years later at 511 South West Street, and customers would endure long waits for tables at both restaurants, especially on weekends.

As the '90s arrived, though, tastes started to change. The east-side restaurant closed and was turned into a Hometown Buffet restaurant in 1993. The west-side Chi Chi's lasted until June 1999, when Rand Graphics bought the building. The East Central Chi Chi's building is now a party venue owned by Wichita Brewing Company, and the west-side building, which held a series of Asian buffets through the 2000s, was torn down in early 2021 to make way for a new convenience store.

BOMBAY BICYCLE CLUB (1982)

For a time in the 1970s, a restaurant and club called Smuggler's Inn on the outskirts of the brand-new Towne East Square was the place to be for young disco fans. But as the 1980s approached and disco started to die, Smuggler's closed its doors, taking with it the youthful memories of a generation of *Saturday Night Fever* fans.

In December 1982, a new business took over the space at 7700 East Kellogg. Bombay Bicycle Club was one of a chain of restaurants owned by Associated Hosts of Beverly Hills, which had also owned Smuggler's

Inn. It was a private restaurant that would become a favorite among the next generation of stylish young people: the yuppies of the 1980s. After it first opened and well into the 1980s, Bombay Bicycle Club was wall-to-wall people on Friday nights, a place where stylish singles mingled. In a 1985 *Wichita Eagle* story about the rise of yuppie culture, the restaurant's manager, Stein Hunter, said that owners of Bombay Bicycle Club advertised it as the place to be seen in town. "Yuppie is an attitude, a state of mind," he said. "Anything you can do to tie into that state of mind will bring those people to you."

The interior design was typical of the day: wooden floors, lots of plant life and windows covered with venetian blinds. The menu was filled with things like steak, fried shrimp and pasta. The Monte Cristo sandwich was a big seller, and the yuppies also loved their chicken salads made with walnuts.

By the 1990s, the restaurant was no longer quite as popular, and it seemed to have the type of identity crisis that signals the end for an aging chain. In 1992, it launched a new menu that focused on Indian, Caribbean, Chinese and Japanese dishes, though it kept many of its original favorites. It appears that the restaurant closed in 1995, and by early 1997, a new-to-Wichita restaurant called Old Chicago had moved into the space.

AMARILLO GRILL (1982)

In 1982, a young restaurateur named Alan Bundy—who had made his career as director of operations for Godfather's Pizza in Wichita—took over the Old Way Station building at 6615 East Central and opened a new restaurant called The Homestead, which specialized in steaks cooked over an open grill filled with mesquite wood. He added a second restaurant at 600 South Holland and had so much success that he expanded into Topeka and Overland Park. That's when Bundy decided to change the restaurants' names to Amarillo Grill.

Business was brisk at the restaurants, which also served fajitas and ribs. Bundy, who also opened Magnolia Cafe in 1986, had a hit on his hands with Amarillo Grill. In 1990, *Wichita Eagle* restaurant critic Diane Lewis gave the East Central restaurant a positive review, saying she loved its T-bone steak and salmon filet and guessing that Wichita would love its generous portions and good service. In 1994, Bundy moved the east-side Amarillo Grill to an easier-to-find spot at 5730 East Central, and two years later, he sold the Amarillo Grill concept to Wichita-based Maverick Restaurant

Corp., which changed the name to Amarillo Mesquite Grill and started an aggressive expansion. By 2000, there were thirteen Amarillo Grills in cities and towns across Kansas and Oklahoma. The company also moved the west-side Wichita restaurant to 8406 Central and opened another Wichita restaurant at 3151 North Rock Road. Bundy remained the restaurants' manager and part owner.

But by 2003, the company declared bankruptcy, citing looming debt and increased competition. All three of the Wichita restaurants were closed by 2004. Bundy bought four Amarillo Grill restaurants outside of Wichita out of bankruptcy and also went on to try out a few new restaurant concepts, including Zyng Noodlery in Old Town Square and Zpizza at 306 North Rock Road. When those didn't work out, he announced plans in 2007 to give Amarillo Grill another try and revived it at 306 North Rock Road. But it lasted only a year.

JOE KELLY'S OYSTER DOCK (1983)

Kansas has never been known for its fresh seafood, for obvious reasons, so any restaurant serving it always captures attention. That was particularly true in 1983, when the new restaurant all the meat-and-potatoes eaters in Wichita were talking about was Joe Kelly's Oyster Dock. It was to be opened on the edges of Towne East Square by Kelly-Johnston, the same company responsible for bringing Chi Chi's to town. Joe Kelly's address was 7700 East Kellogg, but it bordered Douglas, and it opened in December of that year—almost a year and a half after Wichita's first Red Lobster opened on West Street. Its newly constructed building had 8,200 square feet with sweeping windows offering a view…of the mall's parking lot. The restaurant had other decorative touches that gave it the air of a seaside eatery, though, including an outdoor walkway lined with ropes that resembled an ocean dock. When it opened in 1983, the *Wichita Eagle* described it as treading "a fine line between a fern bar and fine restaurant."

Joe Kelly's had a *U*-shaped dining room situated around a bar and dim lighting, and its menu boasted the type of fish dishes health-conscious diners were demanding at the time, including poached sockeye salmon. The menu also offered shrimp, scallops, lobster and oysters on the half shell as well as steaks and pasta dishes. Joe Kelly's was a hit in Wichita for twenty years, but it closed in 2004.

CAFE CHANTILLY (1983)

The year was 1983, and Lebanese immigrant Antoine Toubia was a young Wichita restaurateur on the rise. He'd opened his popular Olive Tree four years earlier, where he'd introduced meat-and-potatoes-loving Wichitans to things like quiche and crepes. And he'd just purchased a bakery and café called Bagatelle that would allow him to supply his restaurant with fresh-baked bread. That's when Toubia took over an old Kip's Big Boy building at 6921 East Kellogg and turned it into Cafe Chantilly—an eclectic eatery that would become one of his most remembered ventures.

Toubia, who would go on to found several Wichita restaurants that he grouped under the company name Latour, pitched Cafe Chantilly as a European-style bistro. He hung lace curtains and painted the walls peach. The floors were terrazzo, the ceilings were high and the dining room was filled with bamboo chairs and tables covered in white tablecloths. The tables were set with fan-shaped napkins, and the room was full of lush plant life. Cafe Chantilly's menu featured "continental" dishes made with chicken, beef and fish—entrées like beef filet with a peppercorn and brandy sauce, grilled salmon with a tomato and cilantro sauce, lamb shanks and a popular chicken moutarde. The menu, which changed with the seasons, also featured salads, sandwiches and pasta dishes, and a deli case at the entrance was stuffed with French pastries and desserts like lemon charlotte and chocolate genoise.

Ten years after it opened, Cafe Chantilly's lease was up, and Kellogg expansion was threatening the space anyway. Toubia announced that he would close the restaurant in August 1993. Fans were distraught and begged him to reconsider. They called and wrote letters, and Toubia even received a petition with five hundred signatures asking him not to close. Toubia admitted he would miss the restaurant, too, and told the *Wichita Eagle* he estimated that he'd served more than one million

Cafe Chantilly, one of Antoine Toubia's early restaurants, opened at 6921 East Kellogg in 1983. *From the* Wichita Eagle.

The interior of Cafe Chantilly, which Antoine Toubia opened in 1983. *Latour.*

diners during the decade it was open. But he had other businesses to keep him busy. By then, he'd added Chelsea's Bar & Grill and Piccadilly Market to his collection.

Two years later, Toubia was diagnosed with cancer of the esophagus, and he died at home in July 1996. He was forty-seven. Today, his two sisters, brother and nephew still run Latour restaurant group, which includes a big catering operation, two restaurants and several cafés within other businesses.

LONGNECKERS (1984)

Longneckers was an Oklahoma City–based gourmet burger chain that billed itself as an alternative to fast food. The chain landed in Wichita in 1984 and made an impression.

Local lawyer L.D. Klenda and his son, Larry, were the Longneckers franchisees in Wichita. They opened their first restaurant in Plaza Del Sol at 535 North Woodlawn, and it specialized in oversized half-pound burgers served on buns made in-house. Customers could top the burgers with anything they wanted to grab from a well-stocked condiment bar that included everything from mustard and ketchup to sauerkraut and specialty sauces. The menu also featured curly fries, chili, ribeye steak sandwiches and milkshakes. It also served, of course, long-necked bottles of beer.

People waiting to order could see raw beef quarters hanging from hooks in a separate room, driving home the idea that the beef was fresh. The staff included both a butcher and a baker. The dining room featured tables covered with checkered tablecloths, and the walls were lined with green

Longneckers was a gourmet hamburger chain popular in Wichita in the 1980s. Pictured here in the restaurant in 1984 are owner Larry Klenda (*left*) and operations director Troy Meier. *From the* Wichita Eagle.

and red neon. People ordered their food at the counter and then waited to pick it up.

The Klendas added a second Longneckers at 1140 West Pawnee in July 1985. Another opened at 630 Robin, near Central and Tyler, in 1986 and another at 2626 South Rock Road in 1988. But as the 1980s progressed, the restaurants started to close, starting with the Pawnee and Robin stores in 1989 and followed by the Woodlawn and South Rock Road restaurants in 1990.

Unrelated owners bought the Longneckers name in 1990 and reopened the original restaurant at 535 North Woodlawn as a New York–style deli selling bagels, burgers, kosher corned beef and pastrami. It lasted about three years.

YEN CHING (1985)

Modern-day Wichitans best remember the Yen Ching that operated at 430 North Rock Road and closed in 2014 after three decades of serving

Wichitans addictive sizzling rice soup, pu pu platters and Chinese delicacies. But Wichita's first Yen Ching opened at 303 East Pawnee in early 1985. Yen Ching 2, as the Rock Road restaurant was called, quickly followed in August 1985, and there was even a third Yen Ching, which briefly operated at 631 North Ridge Road starting in 1986. The original Yen Ching owner in Wichita was Key Liu, who had learned to cook in South Korea. He offered buffets at the west and south locations and advertised that his restaurants served a large variety of Chinese, Mandarin and Szechuan fare. By 1990, the Rock Road Yen Ching was the only one still operating, run by Tom Chang. Over the next decade, Yen Ching became one of Wichita's top Chinese restaurants.

The Rock Road location had two levels, and downstairs, customers loved the floor-to-ceiling booths that allowed for lots of privacy. The dining room had seating for 150 and a menu that offered more than sixty entrées, many of them served spicy. People especially loved Yen Ching's pu pu platter, which included egg rolls, shrimp tempura, crab Rangoon, seasoned chicken and grilled beef, and the waiters would prepare moo shu dishes tableside. The Rock Road Yen Ching remained a Wichita favorite until 2014, when Tom Chang and his wife, Cathay, lost the lease on their space, whose owner planned to demolish it to make way for a new Qdoba restaurant. The couple took some time off to travel, and in 2016, they opened a new quick-service Chinese restaurant at 2431 North Greenwich called Tasty House.

WILLIE C'S (1985)

In 1985, Bill Rowe and some partners opened the first Willie C's Cafe on the perimeter of Towne East Square, right next door to Joe Kelly's Oyster Dock. The 230-seat restaurant was going to be a fun place, Rowe said, with a nostalgia-inspired décor and a menu featuring the type of blue plate specials he grew up eating in small-town cafés. Soon everyone was talking about the restaurant—and everyone was going there for chicken fried steak, burgers and malts. The first Willie C's address was 7700 East Kellogg, though it was closer to Douglas. It became famous for a lifelike policeman on a motorcycle peeking out from behind a billboard, a persuasive prank that would cause many motorists to hit the brakes. Sales were strong, and just three years later, Rowe announced plans to add a second Willie C's, this one on the west side. It opened at Kellogg and West in April 1989 with its own nostalgic flair. Built with a 1940s gas station feel, it even had old gas pump replicas situated out front. The interior was decorated with old advertising signs, taxidermied animals and antique toys. It seated 100 in the dining room and another 50 in the bar, and people would crowd in for Cobb salads, baked potato soup, barbecue ribs and more.

Both Wichita restaurants became dining destinations for Wichitans and people from nearby small towns, and in the mid-1990s, Rowe added Willie C's restaurants in Topeka, Lawrence and St. Joseph, Missouri. The out-of-town restaurants were all closed by the late 1990s, and the east-side Willie C's followed in the fall of 2000. Rowe cited increased competition for the restaurants' decline, though in 2001, he said that the Willie C's at 656 South West Street was still profitable. That remained true for only another few years. Rowe became frustrated with the West Street location, which he said had good lunch business but was dead at dinnertime because of the lack of homes nearby. He initially announced plans to look for a new location, but in 2008, he closed the last Willie C's and bought another popular local restaurant—Red Bean's Bayou Grill—from restaurateur Richard Waite. Though he closed Red Bean's in 2014, Rowe still owns his Blue Moon Caterers business and has been known to occasionally put on popular events where he revives recipes from both Willie C's and Red Bean's menus.

MAGNOLIA CAFE (1986)

Wichita was pretty excited when, in December 1986, restaurateur and Amarillo Grill founder Alan Bundy partnered with Pizza Hut co-founder Dan Carney to open a new restaurant specializing in Cajun-Creole cuisine. He named it Magnolia Cafe, and he put it at 6411 East Central, right on the corner of Central and Woodlawn. At the time, Cajun fare was experiencing a surge in popularity, fueled by cookbook author and chef Paul Prudhomme, who owned Paul's Louisiana Kitchen in New Orleans. And the look of Wichita's new Cajun restaurant was certainly New Orleans inspired. The exterior was painted pink with green window frames and shutters. Inside, there was seating for 102, and the design included dark green carpets and pale green walls with darker pink accents. Jazz posters hung on the walls of the dining room, which was separated into two sections, and the restaurant was decorated with stained-glass panels featuring images of magnolias.

Wichitans also loved the New Orleans–style menu, which was said to offer the spiciest food in town. Dishes included boiled crawfish, blackened redfish, seafood gumbo, etouffee and shrimp creole. Magnolia Cafe was famous for a salad dressing called Hazel dressing, named for a Cajun cook, managers said. It was a creamy tomato dressing spiked with pieces of green onion, but the recipe was a guarded secret. (It did not, however, include hazelnuts, despite many patrons mistakenly dubbing the dressing "hazelnut.")

The first signs of trouble at Magnolia Cafe arrived in May 1993, when owners announced that they were permanently adding Caribbean fare to the menu and added a faux palm tree to the dining room to reflect the new direction. A year later, Magnolia Cafe was closed, and owners replaced it with a new concept called Charlie Tango's Seafood Grill and BarBQ. Bundy told the *Wichita Eagle* at the time that the menu was more mainstream than Magnolia Grill's and would appeal to a

Magnolia Cafe was a popular Cajun-Creole restaurant opened by Alan Bundy in 1986. *From the Wichita Eagle.*

wider audience. But Charlie Tango's didn't last long and was permanently closed by October 1995. A Spangles now operates on the site.

THOSE CRAZY LIQUOR LAWS, PART II

The liquor-by-the-drink question made it to the ballot again in 1986, and Kansas voters finally approved a constitutional amendment repealing the state's ban on open saloons. The measure passed 64 percent to 35 percent, and businesses where food made up 30 percent of sales would soon be able to start serving drinks without memberships. When the voters approved the change on November 4, 1986, Kansas was one of the last three states where liquor by the drink could not be served in public places. The change was beneficial to many restaurants and changed the type of food-and-drink businesses that would open going forward.

When the law took effect in July 1987, several restaurants, including Scotch & Sirloin and Bombay Bicycle Club, celebrated with promotions. The Scotch donated a quarter to charity for each club card turned in. It also sold T-shirts featuring the image of a club card in a circle with a slash through it and the date July 1, 1987. A month later, a story in the *Wichita Eagle* said that many restaurant owners were reporting a surge in sales, including Angelo Fasciano, founder of Angelo's Italian restaurant, and Sonny Glennon of Tom & Sonny's, who said revenue was up 10 percent. Kay Shibley, owner of Kamiel's, told the paper he was glad he could finally "operate our business like human beings."

LAKIS PLACE (1987)

Wichita has long been home to lots of Mediterranean restaurants. But one specific type of Mediterranean cuisine locals always say they wish the city had is traditional Greek. Over the years, a few authentic Greek restaurants have existed. The longest running and best remembered might have been Lakis Place, a tiny hole-in-the-wall that lasted from 1987 until the early 2000s at 3218 South Oliver.

It was owned by Pantelis "Lakis" Agathanglidis, who for two years before he opened Lakis had run The Gyro Place at First and Washington. He moved when his building was scheduled for demolition. The South Oliver restaurant, which operated in the shadow of what was then Boeing, had room enough for only ten chrome tables, which were lined with mismatched chairs. Lakis had posters of Greece on the walls and piped Greek music into the dining room.

His menu was also small and consisted of gyros, souvlaki, lemon chicken, Greek salad and burgers. The gyro meat was rotating on a spit, and Lakis would shave it thin and grill it before serving it to his hungry customers with a side of lemony potatoes. He was also known for his baklava, which the *Wichita Eagle* noted in 1989 was "especially wonderful: much more pecans and sugar syrup than it is pastry and butter."

The owner, who worked alone in the restaurant, was also a bit of a character. His clothes were rumpled, and he was quick to share his opinions on any number of subjects. But Wichita loved his food and frequently declared it was the best Greek food they'd ever had. The restaurant appears to have lasted until about 2005. Then Da Cajun Shak founder Tim Granger took the building over and opened a restaurant serving another cuisine that Wichitans craved but could rarely find.

LE BEAUJOLAIS (1987)

Bob Goehring was a Wichita kid who grew up with a travel bug. He spent time in France and fell in love with the cuisine, ultimately deciding he wanted to be a chef. He went to New York City to attend Peter Kump's New York Cooking School, which he'd learned in the *New York Times* was one of the best. Upon returning home, he had a brief stint at a country club before he "took a dive" and opened a little restaurant where he could practice his craft on a live audience. He leased a space in the back of Clifton Square, a little collection of converted old houses in Wichita's College Hill neighborhood that was home to several different businesses, and in 1987, he opened Le Beaujolais. "I just wanted to bring some of the food of France to Wichita," remembered Goehring, who today lives in Grand Rapids, Michigan.

The restaurant, which operated in the space where Dempsey's Burger Pub is today, served French fare prepared by Goehring. He'd offer a rotating menu featuring four or five entrées each week, things like shrimp Provençal, filet of beef with Burgundy wine sauce or something made with

The interior of Le Beaujolais, a popular French restaurant Bob Goehring opened in Clifton Square in 1987. *Painting by Jim Bartz.*

veal, sweetbreads, lamb or game. A small standard menu that didn't change included things like French onion soup and several desserts. People went crazy for the restaurant's lemon mousse and Goehring's Queen of Sheba cake, a dense creation made with dark chocolate and chocolate glaze. The restaurant also was known for its wine list, which included 120 different bottles. Goehring would often throw a party in November celebrating the annual arrival of Beaujolais Nouveau wine, his restaurant's namesake.

Inside, there was room for just forty people at a time. The dining room featured an antique mantelpiece, lace curtains and fresh flowers on the tables. There was also an intimate area that held a table for two, screened off with an old oak and etched glass door. Wichita didn't have anything like it at the time, and the restaurant was an instant hit with the local food-and-wine crowd. "We had a nice little following," Goehring said.

Over time, though, Goehring got burned out. He did all the cooking himself, and in retrospect, he acknowledged he probably should have relinquished a little bit of control over the place. He sold Le Beaujolais to Mon Yee in 1989, but it closed in May 1991, with the new owner citing poor walk-in business. Goehring would go on to work in another country club and then got into wine sales.

Today, he said, he looks back on the restaurant as a happy blip in his life. He made good friends and good memories and made a mark on the Wichita dining scene. "I've had people tell me, 'We weren't going to move to Wichita. Then we came to your restaurant and realized we could,'" he said. "That made me feel good."

PASTA MILL (1988)

In 1988, Wichita's now-thriving Old Town district was still a new concept and mostly just a collection of decaying warehouses. There were only three restaurants to choose from—The Beacon, Old Mill Tasty Shop and newcomer Rock Island Cafe—and none of them attracted business past lunchtime. When former Pizza Hut employee Gary Streepy opened Pasta Mill at 808 East Douglas in early 1988, he did so hoping to attract an after-hours clientele. And it worked.

The restaurant focused on dishes that used fresh pasta the restaurant made on-site. Inside, it was decorated with a flour mill theme that included framed flour sacks on the walls, green carpet and exposed brick. The dining room could seat 120, and the tables and chairs were made from oak. A

Gary Streepy opened Pasta Mill in Old Town in 1988 and proved that a dinner restaurant could work in the burgeoning downtown district. *Gary Streepy.*

Pasta Mill served fresh pasta made on-site. *Gary Streepy.*

separate lounge featured a twenty-four-foot cherry bar that had once been used at the Eaton Hotel tavern.

In addition to about twenty-four different pasta dishes like sausage manicotti, cheese tortellini and lasagna, the menu featured appetizers, soups and sub sandwiches. Pasta dishes were served with a side salad, and diners had to be careful not to overindulge on complimentary breadsticks before the meals arrived. People would top their pasta dishes with fresh Parmesan cheese using the graters left on each table. And Pasta Mill also sold wine. The restaurant was extremely popular for several years and even expanded to add a meeting room and more dining space in 1989. Streepy also opened a west-side Pasta Mill at 8442 West Thirteenth in 1990 but closed it ten months later. The downtown Pasta Mill closed in August 1994, and Streepy pointed to heavy competition from other restaurants and bars that appeared after he opened, including the much larger Spaghetti Warehouse that opened nearby in 1993. Plus, his lease was up, and rental rates were rising as the Old Town district continued to catch on. But Pasta Mill is to this day considered one of Old Town's most significant pioneers, a restaurant that showed other budding entrepreneurs that an eatery could attract crowds downtown, even after work hours. Restaurant and bar Emerson Biggins has occupied the old Pasta Mill space in Wichita since 1999.

Still Serving after All These Years

It's natural to want to pay homage to the dozens of Wichita restaurants that over the years have opened, earned legions of fans and then closed, destined to live only in old photographs and in customers' memories. But Wichita also has a rather large crop of restaurants that are somehow still open after more than 50 years. One can even trace its roots back more than 110 years.

It wouldn't be right not to include in this book the iconic Wichita restaurants that started generations ago and have managed to survive into modern times. Here are some of the most notable:

LIVINGSTON'S. Andy Livingston opened Wichita's first Livingston's restaurant in 1910 at 310 North Emporia—which back in those days was the edge of town. His menu included five-cent hamburgers and ten-cent T-bone steaks. The original Livingston's is long gone, but founder Andy Livingston's great-granddaughter, Melissa Atkinson, owns Livingston's Cafe at 4733 East Douglas. And his grandson Bob's widow, Jeanne Shaft, owns Livingston's Diner at 9747 East Twenty-First Street. There, customers can see a mural depicting a photo of the original café and images of the founders, Andy and Tina Livingston. Both specialize in the type of home-cooking and blue plate specials that the founder would likely have approved of.

NUWAY CAFE. Wichita's oldest restaurant still operating with the same name in its original spot is NuWay Cafe, which has sold loose meat sandwiches at

The first NuWay opened on West Douglas in 1930. It's still operating today. *Neal Stong.*

1416 West Douglas since 1930. Now a Wichita institution with several local locations, NuWay specializes in "crumbly" burgers (best eaten with mustard, pickles and chopped onions only) as well as onion rings and root beer.

Tom McEvoy opened the restaurant in a tiny brick building with room enough only for a standup counter on July 4, 1930. The country was in the middle of the Great Depression, but McEvoy had patented a steam cooker, which he'd used in Iowa to sell loose-meat sandwiches he called Made Rites. When he moved to Wichita, he called them NuWays and sold them for a dime apiece. He ran the restaurant with his wife, Helen, until he died in late 1965. After that, Helen took over and ran NuWay for another decade before retiring, selling the restaurant to Gene Friedman and Jack Freeman. Those two are responsible for starting NuWay's expansion, and four local restaurants still operate. Longtime employee Neal Stong acquired the NuWay chain in 1999 and still runs it. The most popular store is the original, which has been expanded four times since it first opened but still has a retro lunch counter customers love.

OLD MILL TASTY SHOP, 604 East Douglas. German immigrant Otto Woermke and his wife, Erna, opened Old Mill on March 1, 1932, on the

Otto Woermke and his wife, Erna, opened Old Mill Tasty Shop on March 1, 1932. Mary Wright, who owns the restaurant today, bought it in 1982. *John Freeman for the* Wichita Eagle.

corner of Douglas and St. Francis. And it's still in business, serving up blue plate specials from the kitchen and shakes and malts from the soda fountain. Woermke moved the restaurant to its current spot at 604 East Douglas in 1940 and ran the place, always wearing his signature butcher's apron, until he died in 1981. Among his specialties were liverwurst and cheese sandwiches, homemade chili, sundaes and ice cream sodas. Mary Wright took over the restaurant in 1982 and runs it today with her son, Don. Though they still serve ice cream from Old Mill's original marble soda fountain, many of Mary Wright's own recipes have helped the restaurant endure, including her famous chicken salad and green chili.

MERLE'S PLACE, 440 North Seneca. It opened in 1935 as Tom's Inn, just two years after Prohibition ended. Tom and Fern Loup went into business intending to serve beer to the thirsty citizens of Wichita, and Storz Brewing Co. even built them a brand-new mahogany bar. That bar is still in the building at 440 North Seneca, though it's been called Merle's Place since Merle Bates bought it in 1966. Merle's, as regulars call it, is popular for its Reuben sandwiches and shuffleboard table.

SAVUTE'S, 3303 North Broadway. The era that produced swanky north-side restaurants like Abe's, Ken's Klub and Doc's Steakhouse also gave Wichita Savute's. The family-owned Italian restaurant at 3303 North Broadway is the only survivor. Its origins date back to 1943, when first-generation Italian immigrants John and Mary Savute paid $4,000 for a hotel at 3411 North Broadway that had thirteen cabins. They added on a club, calling it The Highway Club, and operated it during a time when North Broadway was full of nightclubs and bootleggers. After a couple of years, they turned the nightclub into an Italian restaurant called Rosie's, moving it to its current location in 1952. John's son, John Jr., eventually took over the restaurant, and he changed its name to Savute's. It was a popular Wichita dining destination in the 1950s and one of the first places in town to serve pizza.

John Jr., who was also a pilot, died in 2001 in a light plane crash in Greenwood County, and his son, Peter, took over the restaurant. He still owns it today, along with an attached aviation-themed club his father founded called Stick 'N Rudder. Though it's open for limited hours, Savute's still has a legion of devoted customers who order its steaks, chicken scallopini, lasagna and pasta dishes.

DOG N SHAKE. A little restaurant called Sizzlin' Dog that opened in 1948 would grow into one of Wichita's longest-running and most-loved fast-food hot dog and burger restaurants—Dog N Shake, which still has four locations in Wichita. Neal Adamson, who in 1954 opened a restaurant at 4323 South Seneca called Neal's Burger Bar, bought Sizzlin' Dog in 1958, and in 1962, he merged the two businesses into the Dog N Shake concept, opening several more over the years. Adamson died in 2001, but his two daughters and granddaughter are still carrying on his legacy, and customers still clamor for Dog N Shake's hot dogs, burgers served on butter-toasted buns, onion rings, chili and shakes.

BOMBER BURGER, 4860 South Clifton. This restaurant first opened in 1952 and for years was known as a honky-tonk bar with good burgers. Paul Rickard bought it in 1985, and his son, Chris—famous for his surly attitude and love of the Pittsburgh Steelers—still runs the tiny burger stand today.

CALVIN'S HAMBURGER HAVEN, 1929 South Seneca. This burger restaurant originally opened in May 1952 in a tiny building at 1526 South Seneca and was a popular hangout for teens. It operated there until 1990, when a new QuikTrip was slated to be built on its spot. The owner took the well-seasoned grill with him when he moved it to its current spot on the end cap of a strip center.

TY'S DINER, 928 West Second Street. Kenny Tyson opened this greasy burger restaurant in 1953, and it's been through a variety of owners, including Vern and Dottie Hartley in the 1980s. Kristin Hale, the restaurant's seventh and current owner, is still serving Ty's famous menu of burgers, chicken strips and fresh-cut fries.

SPEAR'S RESTAURANT AND PIE SHOP, 4323 West Maple. Gene Spear; his wife, Betty; and his mother, Mayme Rasmussen, opened the first Spear's in a converted house at the corner of Mt. Vernon and Oliver in 1956. It was famous for its homemade pies but also served things like sandwiches, roast beef and pumpkin bread with whipped honey. The restaurant operated in the original spot until 1968, when it moved into a big new building to the north. At one time, there were six Spear's restaurants. But only the one on West Maple remains. It's owned by Dan Crandall, a longtime employee who bought Spear's from Randy Spear in 2014.

TOWN & COUNTRY, 4702 West Kellogg. When Jay Conover opened this restaurant in 1957, it wasn't even in the city limits. At that time, the edge of the city was West Street. But Conover decided he'd take over the restaurant attached to the Town & Country Lodge, and it became one of Wichita's most enduring restaurants, offering a menu of home cooking favorites like chicken fried steak and prime rib. Jay's son, Larry, took it over after his father died of esophageal cancer in 1980; then Larry died in 2020 of throat cancer. The restaurant closed at the beginning of the COVID-19 pandemic, shortly after Larry's death, and it looked like it was going to stay that way. Then, some new owners took the building over and reopened it as Town & Country, serving the same menu.

ANGELO'S, 5231 East Central. Angelo and Anna Fasciano started making pizzas out of the basement of their home in the late 1950s, and Angelo—who was born in Sicily—would take them to work at Boeing and sell them to his co-workers. They became so popular that in 1960, he and his wife were able to open a small restaurant, which they called Angelo's, on South Laura. The restaurant moved to Harry and Hillside in 1961 and to a new spot across the street in 1976. But wherever it went, customers followed to get the restaurant's pizzas, homey pasta dishes and salads topped with pickled eggplant.

Over the years, Angelo's expanded, and at one point, there were five Angelo's restaurants in Wichita as well as restaurants in Andover, Hutchinson

Left: Ty's Diner has been in business since 1953. *Painting by Bill Goffrier.*

Below: Town & Country first opened in Wichita in 1957. *Larry Conover.*

Angelo's founder Angelo Fasciano (*right*) is pictured in 1986 with his son and current owner Jack Fasciano. *From the* Wichita Eagle.

and Tulsa. Anna died in 2004, followed by her husband a year later. Their son, Jack, took over, but by 2006, he was out of money and closed the last remaining Angelo's at 1930 South Oliver. Fans spent the next decade dreaming about the restaurant's food, and in 2016, Jack and his daughter, Gina Fasciano Hogan, were able to revive it in a new location at 5231 East Central with the help of a Kickstarter campaign that raised more than $40,000. In the spring of 2021, the restaurant moved again to a bigger space at 5900 East Central.

TACO GRANDE. Some say that Michael "Mike" Foley introduced fast-food tacos to the Midwest when he opened his first Taco Grande restaurant in 1960 at 857 South Oliver. It was a hit, and the restaurant was soon franchised across the nation. Foley, whose cousins Dan and Robin Foley started the Taco Tico chain, held on to the restaurants until 1982, when he retired and moved to California. He died in 2017. Wichita still has two Taco Grande restaurants: one at 2315 West Twenty-First Street North and one at 2255 South Seneca.

TACO TICO. Mike Foley's cousins, Dan Foley and brother Robin, started off in business with Mike but went their own way. In 1962, they opened their first Taco Tico fast-food restaurant at Seneca and Harry, and it caught on. It had expanded to five restaurants by 1967, when it was incorporated. A generation of Wichitans grew up eating the chain's taco burgers, burritos and sanchos, but the chain got into tax trouble in 2013, when the last Wichita store closed. But a new owner, Greg White, reopened the Taco Tico at Thirteenth and Tyler and followed with another in a former Taco Tico building at 460 North West Street four years later. Today, White has three Taco Ticos in Wichita as well as restaurants in El Dorado, Newton, Arkansas City, Derby and Augusta. Though Taco Tico is no longer a franchise, there are still restaurants in several states, including Oklahoma, Texas, Kentucky, Iowa and Louisiana.

This photo of Connie's founders Connie and Ralph Lopez, *standing at left*, was taken in the restaurant in 1984. Connie's first opened in 1963. *Carmen Rosales.*

CONNIE'S MEXICO CAFE, 2227 North Broadway. Wichita's oldest family-run Mexican restaurant was opened in 1963 by Connie and Ralph Lopez, who moved from Texas with their small daughter, Carmen, and took over a space on North Broadway that had previously held a bar called Chata's. That space was right next door to where Connie's operates today. It moved in the early 1970s. Today, the restaurant is run by Carmen Rosales and her daughters, and it's been visited by many famous faces over the years, including then-presidential candidate Jimmy Carter and movie star Harrison Ford. It's known for its friendly service, big beef burritos and fried tacos that have peas and potatoes mixed into the beef filling.

FELIPE'S. Many Wichita Mexican restaurant owners got their starts working at Felipe's, which was founded in February 1967 by Felipe Lujano, who immigrated to the United States from Tepatitlán, Mexico. His restaurant at 3434 West Central caught on, and more and more Felipe's opened over the years. Today, there are four in Wichita, each owned by different members of Lujano's family. He died in 2006, but his grown sons, Felipe Jr. and Poncho, still run two of the Felipe's restaurants with help from their mother, Lucia, including the original on West Central. The restaurants are known for their famous fishbowl-sized drink called The Flaming Cazuela and for their tacos, enchiladas and burritos.

Felipe Lujano Sr. opened the first Felipe's Mexican Restaurant in Wichita in 1967. *Felipe Lujano Jr.*

CRAZY HORSE SUPPER CLUB, 2539 West Pawnee. Sam and Ramona Peabody opened this south-side supper club in 1967, and it became known for its delicacies like frog legs, alligator tail, bull fries and chicken gizzards. Second-shift Cessna workers would also go there to get a good steak. The restaurant, whose recognizable signage featured a hand-drawn unicorn, continued on after Sam Peabody died in 1994 and left the business to his daughters. They ran it for eight or nine more years, but the restaurant was gone by 2004, and a string of other eateries moved into and out of the space. Then, in 2020, Peabody's grandson, Eric, took over the vacant space and revived the restaurant. It's back in business with an updated interior and a menu that includes bull fries, alligator bites and frog legs.

SCOTCH & SIRLOIN, 5325 East Kellogg. Delmar and Rose Kuhlman opened this popular Wichita steakhouse on East Kellogg and Bluff in 1968, and it was one of Wichita's hotspots throughout the 1970s and 1980s. Businessmen took clients they wanted to impress there for lunch. Couples looked forward all year to anniversary dinners there. Known for its dim lighting, good steaks and waitresses in low-cut tops, the restaurant never lost popularity, though in 1997, it did lose its original building to Kellogg expansion. But it took over a larger space nearby at 5325 East Kellogg, where it still operates today. Restaurateur Mike Issa bought "The Scotch" in 2014 and has since completely remodeled the interior into a luxurious, modern showpiece. It remains one of Wichita's most popular business and special occasion destinations.

Sources

Catholic Advance

Hill, Roland P. *I Recommend: Where to Go, Stop, Eat, Play and Shop.* N.p.: De Laney and Company, 1948.

Hung, Wayne Wong. *American Paper Son: A Chinese Immigrant in the Midwest.* Urbana: University of Illinois Press, 2006.

Wichita Beacon

Wichita Daily Leader

Wichita Daily Republican

Wichita Eagle

Wichita Eagle and Beacon

Wichita Opinion

Wichita This Week

Wichita Weekly Beacon

Index

A

Abe's Club 10, 59, 64, 65
Ablah Company, The 37, 48
Ablah, George 47, 96
Aboud, Jim 109, 110
Abraham, Abe and Mabel 64, 65
Abraham, Don 65
Abraham, Ron and Sheriann 64, 65
Adair, Larry 75
Adams Barbecue 68, 120
Adamson, Neal 147
Agathanglidis, Pantellis 139
Albert's Restaurant 10, 60, 61, 62
Amarillo Grill 110, 131, 132, 137
Andeel, Lindy 125
Angelo's 11, 139, 148, 150
Apollo Saloon 16
Applegate's Landing 114, 115
Arcade Restaurant 16
Aronfeld, Lee 122
Auntie Sweet's Bar-B-Que 83
Ayala, Olegario "Horace" 62, 63

B

Bachman, Jim 127, 128
Bagatelle Bakery 126, 133
Bates, Merle 146
Baum, Ralph 51, 52
Beacon, The 141
Big Bun 43, 47, 65, 66
Bill's Le Gourmet 104, 105, 126
Bissantz Bakery 30
Bombay Bicycle Club 130, 131, 139
Bomber Burger 147
Breakfast Club, The 120
Brown, Charley 59, 125
Brown, Richard 56, 58, 59, 125
Brown's Grill 56, 57, 58, 59, 125
Bundy, Alan 110, 131, 132, 137, 138
Burk, Dave 116

C

Cafe Chantilly 10, 126, 133, 134
Calvin's Hamburger Haven 147
Card, Anthony 104
Carney, Dan 84, 85, 137
Carney, Frank 84, 85, 90
Carson, Tom 127

Casey Jones Junction 99, 100
Cedar, The 75, 76
Charley Brown's Restaurant & Lounge
    125
Charlie Tango's Seafood Grill and
    BarBQ 138
Chateau Briand 91, 92
Chelsea's Bar & Grill 126, 127
Chi Chi's 130
Cincinnati Bakery 17
Connie's Mexico Cafe 151
Connoisseur, The 53, 54
Conover, Jay 148
Conover, Larry 148, 149
Continental Grill 43
Crandall, Dan 148
Crazy Horse Supper Club 102, 152
Crestview Country Club 126

D

Da Cajun Shak 139
D'Annunzio, Tom 108, 125
Delmonico Cafe 18
Detroit Dining Parlor 17
Diamond Head 113, 114
Dixie Fried Chicken 38, 40
Dockum Lunch Counter 69
Doc's Steakhouse 73, 74, 147
Dog N Shake 147
Droll, George 41, 49, 50, 51
Droll's English Grill 41, 49, 50, 51
Dr. Redbird's Medicinal Inn 105, 106,
    107, 116
Dry, J. Robert 55
Dry, Verda 55
Dunbar, Mathilda 83
Durant, Harold 43
Dyne Quik 38

E

El Charro Cafe 62, 63
Elizabeth's Restaurant 82, 83

Ellis, Jeanne and Floyd 121, 122
Elpers, Ed 114, 115
Estalita's Tacos 107, 108
Eureka Restaurant 16

F

Fairland Cafe 10, 36, 44, 45
Farha, Doug 125
Fasciano, Angelo and Anna 139, 148,
    150
Fasciano, Jack 150
Felipe's 151
Fife and Drum 10, 89, 90, 112
Foley, Dan 150
Foley, Michael 150
Foley, Robin 150
Forum Cafeteria 34, 80, 81
Frasco, Larry 110, 111
Fred Harvey House 19
Freeman, Jack 145
Friedman, Gene 145

G

Garvie, Annamae 41, 42, 43
Garvie's Restaurant 41, 42, 43
Gatsby's 121, 122
Georgie Porgie Pancake Shop 30, 95,
    96, 97
Glennon, Sonny 108, 125, 139
Goehring, Bob 140, 141
Gourmet 500 113
Grandy's 11, 129, 130
Granger, Don 42
Granger, Tim 139
Grape, The 127, 128
Griff's Burger Bar 91
Grinder Man 37
Gyro Place, The 139

H

Hale, Kristin 148
Hansen, Keith 114
Hartley, Vern and Dottie 148
Harvey, Fred 19, 20
Hatch Cover, The 124, 125
Hickory House 55, 56
Highway Club, The 147
Hill, Ken 59, 60
Hogan, Gina Fasciano 150
Holly Cafe 34, 35, 36
Huey, Elizabeth 82, 83
Hustead, Dwight 73

I

Ichiban 120
Ingram, Billy 26, 27
Innes Tea Room 10, 15, 21, 22, 23
Issa, Mike 125, 152
Italian Garden 125

J

Jabara, Everett 91
Jet Bar-B-Q 90, 112
Joe Kelly's Oyster Dock 132
Judge Riggs 118, 119

K

Kamiel's Restaurant and Club 108, 109
Kau Kau Korner 76, 77, 78
Kellogg 11, 20, 40, 43, 51, 60, 63, 71, 73, 78, 82, 84, 90, 91, 92, 93, 94, 100, 102, 103, 108, 109, 111, 113, 118, 121, 126, 129, 130, 132, 133, 136, 148, 152
Kelly, Kathleen 10, 46, 73, 113, 119
Kelly, Mike 130
Ken's Klub 59, 60, 147
Kentucky Fried Chicken 78
King, A.J. "Jimmie" 28, 45, 46, 47

Kings-X 45, 46, 47, 48
King, Wayne 47, 48
Kip's Big Boy 133
Kistler, Harry 18
Klenda, L.D. and Larry 134, 135
Kretchmar, Bob and Marlys 111
Kuhlman, Delmar 112, 152
Kuhlman, Rose 112, 113, 152
Kwan Court 124, 125

L

Laham, George 95
Lakeshore Club 94, 95, 102
Lakis Place 139
Lancers Club 69, 70, 71
La Palma 90, 112
Larkspur 105, 118
Latour 11, 126, 128, 133, 134
Lazy-R 93, 94
Le Beaujolais 140, 141
Legal Tender Cafe 18
Lettuce Club 122, 123
Lewis, Diane 7, 9, 10, 116, 128, 131
liquor by the drink 102, 138
Livingston, Andy 144
Livingston's 144
Longneckers 134, 135
Looking Glass, The 10, 105, 116, 117
Lopez, Connie and Ralph 151
Loup, Tom and Fern 146
Lujano family 151
Lusk, Bill, Jr. 110

M

Magnolia Cafe 137, 138
Mar, Albert 60
Mar, Chuck 44
Mar, Cornell and Sharon 60, 61
Mar, Gook Poy 34
Mar, King 28, 30
Mar, Tung Jing 28, 30
Mar, Young 79

McEvoy, Tom 145
Mead Building 116
Meeks, Etsuko 120
Meier, Troy 135
Miller, Anthony 92
Miller Theatre 22, 41, 43, 51, 109
Mr. Dunderbak's 112, 113

N

Neal's Burger Bar 147
Nicholson, Rudy and Ruth 94
NuWay Cafe 11, 144, 145

O

Old Chicago 131
Old Mill Tasty Shop 11, 141, 145
Old Town 11, 90, 116, 129, 132, 141, 143
Old Way Station, The 109, 110
Olive Tree 126, 127
Osterhout, Mike 110

P

Pan-American Cafe 28, 29, 30
Papa John's 85
Pasta Mill 141, 142, 143
Peabody, Eric 152
Peabody, Sam and Ramona 152
Pell, Burton 110
Peoples' Restaurant 18
PepsiCo 85
Piccadilly Grill 126
Pit's Bar-B-Q 66, 67, 68
Pizza Hut 11, 69, 84, 85, 90, 114, 115, 130, 137, 141
Polar Bear 38, 39, 40
Portobello Road 83, 102, 110, 111
Private Club Act of 1965, The 102

R

Ralph Baum's Burgers 51, 52
R&S Bar-B-Q 120, 121
Rasmussen, Mayme 148
Ray, Charles and Hattie 120, 121
Reaves, Bill 104, 105
Red Bean's Bayou Grill 94, 137
Reyes, German and Fabiola 112
Rice, T.J. 23, 24, 25, 26
Rickard, Chris 147
Rickard, Paul 147
Rock Island Cafe 141
Rock Road 28, 48, 59, 91, 92, 108, 112, 118, 124, 126, 127, 132, 135, 136
Rosales, Carmen 151
Rowe, Bill 136
Rudy's BBQ 94

S

Sac Souk 126
Sandy's Drive-In 90, 91
Savute, John and Mary 147
Savute, John Jr. 147
Savute, Peter 147
Savute's 11, 59, 73, 147
Schnitzler/Snitzler, Fritz 15, 16
Schoenhofer, Charles "Chuck" 76, 77, 78
Schoenhofer, Denis 78
Scotch & Sirloin 102, 108, 112, 125, 139, 152
Seneca Square Shopping Center 114
Shakey's Pizza Parlor 11, 92, 93
Shibley, Kay 108, 139
Shibley, Patrick and Timirie 108
Sidman, Jack 71, 72, 73
Sidman's 71, 72, 73
Silverman, Mark 127, 128
Sizzlin' Dog 147
Smith, Estalita 107
Smith, Tom 108
Smuggler's Inn 130

South City Restaurant 36
Spear, Gene and Betty 148
Spear, Randy 148
Spear's Restaurant and Pie Shop 148
Sport Burger 37, 51
Steak and Ale 11, 102, 103, 104
Stevens, George, Jr. 93, 94
Stevens, Hugh 76, 77, 78
Stevens, Jim 78
Stong, Neal 145
Streepy, Gary 141, 142, 143
Sun, Barbara and Mark 122
Swiss Colony Inn 97, 98

T

Taco Grande 150
Taco Tico 150
Terradyne Country Club 105
T.J. Rice's Cafeteria 15, 23, 24, 25, 26
Toc's Coffeehouse 47
Tommy's 108, 125
Tom's Inn 146
Tom & Sonny's 108, 125, 139
Torline, M. Eugene 99, 100
Toubia, Antoine 126, 134
Toubia, Joumana 127
Toubia, Randa 127
Town & Country 148
Towne East Square 98, 112, 113, 114, 130, 132, 136
Towne West Square 98
Twin Lakes Shopping Center 97, 98, 106
Two Olives 127
Ty's Diner 149
Tyson, Kenny 148

V

Valentine, Arthur 37, 38
Valentine Diners 37, 38
Vliet, Rich and Marni 105, 106, 107, 116, 117

W

Waite, Richard 137
Werts, Tom and Ted 75
West-Urn, the 48, 49
White Castle 11, 26, 27, 28, 37, 45, 46, 91
White, Greg 150
White Way Recreation 116
White, Willie 66, 67
Wichita State University 56, 75, 84, 120
Willie C's 136, 137
Wishbone Building 89, 90, 112
Woermke, Otto and Erna 145, 146
Wolf, Arthur 34
Wolf, Ernest 30
Wolf's Cafeteria 30, 31, 32, 33, 34
Wong, Ed 30, 96
Wong, Edward 96
Wong, Larry Mark 35
Wong, Wayne 95, 96
Wright, Mary 146
Wright, Seth 38, 40

X

Xidis, Steve and Pat 89, 90

Y

Yen Ching 135, 136
Young, Sai 44

Z

Ziggies 118

About the Author

Denise Neil has worked at the *Wichita Eagle* since late 1997, writing stories for the features, lifestyle and entertainment sections. She started reviewing restaurants and writing about Wichita's dining scene in 2000, and her stories are among the newspaper's most well read. She is a regular speaker around town, and groups who invite her love to hear about where to eat and to reminisce about old favorites. Denise, a Dodge City native and a 1995 graduate of the University of Kansas, also worked at the *Chattanooga Times* and has worked as an adjunct professor of journalism at Newman University in Wichita since the early 2000s. She lives in Wichita with her husband and their two daughters, Alexis and Helen, and loves cooking, traveling and audiobooks.